CONSIDER THIS
ON THIS DAY

More books by Robin K. Johnson

My Spiritual Journal
The Heritage Tree: planted by mom, dad & the girls
Planting Daisies: when roses just won't do !
A Daughter's Book of Secrets

Forthcoming

Clay Castles (2017)

CONSIDER THIS
ON THIS DAY

10 Minute Applicable Bible Lessons
for People on the Go

Robin K. Johnson

Foreword by
Roger S. Nam

RESOURCE *Publications* • Eugene, Oregon

CONSIDER THIS ON THIS DAY
10 Minute Applicable Bible Lessons for People on the Go

Copyright © 2016 Robin K. Johnson. All rights reserved. Except for brief quotations in critical publications or reviews, no part of this book may be reproduced in any manner without prior written permission from the publisher. Write: Permissions, Wipf and Stock Publishers, 199 W. 8th Ave., Suite 3, Eugene, OR 97401.

Resource Publications
An Imprint of Wipf and Stock Publishers
199 W. 8th Ave., Suite 3
Eugene, OR 97401

www.wipfandstock.com

PAPERBACK ISBN: 978-1-4982-8217-8
HARDCOVER ISBN: 978-1-4982-8219-2
EBOOK ISBN: 978-1-4982-8218-5

Manufactured in the U.S.A.   DECEMBER 21, 2016

To Connie and Callie
for being the Godly women you are

FOREWORD
ten minutes a day

ROBIN JOHNSON IS A pastor, teacher, doctoral student, devoted husband, and a father of seven daughters and a son. Robin knows busy. He knows that asking for ten minutes is a sacred request in the middle of a frantic life.

Robin knows that life is both physically but also spiritually frantic as well. So, in asking for ten mere minutes, he gives much more in return. His own frantic life has produced much laughter, and tears as well. His book is a reflection of all of his experiences through Scripture. Younger readers will be introduced to a newfound theological depth. Other readers will see familiar passages like Psalms 8, or Philippians 4, through fresh perspectives of a life filled with joy and some sorrow too. As I read the pages of this book, I am reminded of yet another identity of Robin as a theological student at graduate seminary. He respected the Scriptures so much, that he never hesitated to ask difficult questions and gave himself permission to be troubled and disturbed by the Word of God. But above all, Robin held fast to an underlying belief that somehow, deep within the mysteries of God, the Bible was authoritative, and powerful, and comfortable, and cutting as a two-edged sword.

Robin was an ideal seminary student in many ways. By putting his thoughts to print, he becomes your fellow-traveler, in reflecting on life's franticness through God's word. This reflection is not merely nostalgic, but a springboard for deep spiritual living in the future.

He does not offer easy answers when life confronts Scripture. But Robin does offer empathy as your fellow-traveler, encouragement from his deep pastoral well, and occasionally stern advice (sometime even using

ALL CAPS!) that befits his identity as a father filled with discipline, grace, and love.

So read on, and expect to find empathy, encouragement, advice. Come to think of it, this is quite a return for a mere ten minutes a day.

Dr. Roger S. Nam, PhD.

PREFACE

Living in a society which pushes the spiritual growth of an individual to the brink of breaking down and giving up, there are those moments which one must take pause and reflect on the past and what is required to take assured steps toward success. The Monday through Friday lessons will allow the reader to take an objective look at the various situations and circumstances which can cause enough distraction and force us to miss out on hearing from God.

The lessons contained in Consider This on This Day are not designed for historical information, but short lessons that hone the concept of biblical application and life lessons into short readings which give varied take on the delivery of the text and how an individual can regroup and head back into their daily grind.

We all know that God requires us to give Him a portion of those things we have been blessed with. So, the cause of this book is to answer the call of Matthew 6:33. By giving God 10 minutes of your day, you fulfill those steps when the text asks you to SEEK the Lord.

—Robin K. Johnson

This book is dedicated to the hard-working people at Bay Area Turning Point

www.bayareaturningpoint.org

BATP is a non-profit; community based social service agency providing a variety of assistance services, including shelter,
to families in need and
community education/
crime prevention activities in
Domestic Violence

If you feel moved, please
donate $15.00 to BATP or a Women's Abuse Center in your area.

Monday

Be prepared to be moved in one direction or another

CONSIDER THIS ON THIS DAY

say what you think

When we look at nature, we can see the flows of the rivers and lakes as they are moved by the winds and storms. Sometimes, we can see that there are storms which arise and cause tumultuous patterns to take place in some areas of the lakes and rivers and not others.

Those patterns which are viewed are true to their nature and design.

Then if we look at the nature of the human animal, the people we know and deal with on a day to day basis, we can see in them that there are certain patterns, events and situations that are not naturally occurring but caused by outside sources which may or may not be true to their original design.

These are the people we try hard to love and admire because of their tenacity to speak out on some things and stir up "mess" at work and at church. But to marvel at these antics is too feed into silliness and stupidity. These are those people who are mad all the time for no particular reason. They are just mad and they work situations until the peaceful flow of someone's day is in a storm.

In the 6th chapter of Proverbs, the writer lists six things which God detests and makes no concessions as to a remedy showing that any portion will be accepted through grace. The exampled person listed in these verse, we all know and steer away from. For the most part, we tend to seek them out because it is human nature to watch another make a fool out of someone else. Some may say curiosity. Some may say it is being adventurous. But in all accounts, it is murder. It is spiritual character assassination. It is an open act to destroy the self-esteem of another.

Yet we are amused by these negative actions. Why?

In the 26th chapter of Proverb, the writer gets to the heart of the character of a lying gossip. In the text, we find that the characteristics of this person, is the same characteristics which reside within the lives of someone who has committed the act of physically murdering someone. The difference when it is carried out by the mouth of a Christian is that the gossip is performed over and over and over; repeatedly striking life-ending blows to someone who may be trying to live a life for Christ.

The strangest thing I noticed in these scriptures is that it all takes place in the assembly of the children of God. In other words, it takes place in the church. This makes me know that there are some people we need not associate with in any concept of the word—fellowship.

The seven things that God hates are an abomination to Him and gossip is the chief of the tribe. Say what you will about someone, but it is not hard to consider the fact that those things passed on as a truth, when knowing them to be a lie is gossiping. Gossip is a sin. It is a distraction from hearing from God. It a growing barrier from receiving blessings which have been waited on and not delivered because simple, hateful words are the enemy of a righteous heart.

> Read Proverbs 6:16–19 and Proverbs 26:20–28

Make this day the day you choose not to buy into the stories which come from those folks we know have contentious hearts and devise ways to keep the confusion rising in the church and then in your family.

Rise above the fray. Let your light shine so other can see Christ in all your actions.

CONSIDER THIS ON THIS DAY

a new thing—a new day

Ups and downs, heartaches and heartbreaks, the loss of a loved one and then the loss of a job; these are all things which somehow leaves markers in our memories which are very difficult to pass up when thinking over all those moments of success and gain. As it is said, with every step of success, some tears must fall.

Complacency seems to have its place in our days. We tend to become affixed on the knowledge that we have overcome and have outdone and out maneuvered those obstacles which could have caused us to lose our desire and hope for being successful in love, work and becoming a better person.

But none of this could have been garnered without the Hands of the Lord being in our lives, right?

In Isaiah 43:19, the Lord speaks to His children in open terms and desires them (us) to realize that there need to think on the things of the past as if they are going to somehow reoccur and make us start over again. There is not one day that we can say is exactly as the day before. No circumstance is the same after you've given it thought and have decided to have a conversation with the Lord about it.

We have a God who, if we listen, is constantly speaking to us and He has a deep desire to have us happy and joyous in our successes as long as we are willing to accept the fact that we all belong to Him. Those things which we think as being hard and difficult paths to take, well those have alReady been forged ahead of us (Proverbs 3:5–7).

If we focus on the heartaches, pangs and pains of life and the loss of numerous things we begin to lose focus on the path before us. We begin to stop living and become resemblant of the past. We begin to fade from existence because our friends and family, no matter how much they love us, they will move on and live and walk in the knowledge that each day is a new day and the Lord will affect each of us differently in those new days

So, raise your head up and drop the weights of the past and then breathe.

From the beginning of this chapter, God offers hope, security and the knowledge that we are never out of His Protective Hands (Isa 43:1–2). So, after you Read the first those verses, take confidence in knowing that your faith in the Lord will not be returned to you because God has failed you in any way.

Read Isaiah 43:1–21

Make this day the day you stand up and look at those things which seem to be a challenge in your life and begin to walk in authority. You belong to the Most High God—there is no one on this earth who can take away those things God has meant to be in your life as a blessing and for you for those who are in your circle of influence

CONSIDER THIS ON THIS DAY

words hurt

"STICKS AND STONES MAY break my bones..."

A simple adage used to promote self-esteem and self-worth.

But when you think of the damage done when hurtful and negative words are delivered to the ones you love, while professing to be a Christian delivers a punch that damages the soul and tarnishes your witness.

Those things done in negative actions can never be removed or rewritten. Apologizing is too late because the seed is alReady given and most times, planted within our children who carry this mess as gospel and deliver it to their friends and then into the lives of their own children,

We should do better if we are to gift our children a greater inheritance.

In James 3, words are not watered down in the description of how "fake" some folks can be when it comes to walking the brighter lines of granting love and hope into the daily lives of those around us and those who learn from our every actions. And at the same times, we want God to give us the best He has to offer the world.

No matter how right you are in the conversation, saying things which you know will hurt a person's heart, destroy any portion of their self-esteem and makes you feel powerful is not righteous by any form of the word righteous. At this point, does this make them see the Christ with is supposed to be within you?

If you agree with the following statement, "I am the same person I used to be. I can still show them the old me to get my point across", then something is definitely, defiantly wrong in your fellowship with Christ (II Corinthians 5:17).

CONSIDER THIS ON THIS DAY

We all must do better if we are to make this short journey in life Christ-like.

Read James 3:1–10

Make this day the day you decide to be positive in all actions; work, home & school. Let your light shine so others can truly see Christ in you.

CONSIDER THIS ON THIS DAY

move on & live

Life is hard enough without some folks working daily to remind you of your failures, falters, bad choices and old sin-filled life. These are the same people you wonder, if they are ever going to grow up or come to a better knowledge of what the process of Salvation is.

Romans 8:1–14 sheds light on the issues a Believer must deal with, the flesh & the spirit. In the flesh—the Believer must deal with Earthly desires & the enemies of God. In the Spirit, one has to deal with the issues of giving up and allowing the Holy Spirit to lead, guide and give daily protections.

These are a constant battle. Then we must deal with decisions on who to trust, God or the friend we have grown up with and have allowed to become our mind of reason, when they are in the same negative cycle.

How can we take advice from people who have no power or control on the rising & setting of the Sun? Why do we listen to the so intensely? How many times have you been praying and God shouts into your soul, "you are sorry & worthless"?

You do the math.

Who has failed you more, friends or Christ Jesus & who can offer you "better" days if you call and open your heart and fully give your trust?

make this day the day you decide to move on from your past and trust in God for the increase?

CONSIDER THIS ON THIS DAY
running downhill

IF YOU HAVE EVER taking the time to watch kids play with a box on a hill and how they sat on top of the hill, in that box, rocking back and forth with laughter and smiles to force enough momentum to overcome the gravity stopping it from sliding down to the bottom; it makes you long for your own youthful days.

But if we take a step back and realize that the moment the box starts sliding, no one in the box is in control and all things whizzing by are left open to Murphy's Law. Then we notice that there are more children at the bottom of the hill waiting for their opportunity to enjoy what's inside the box.

Such is our lives. Up and down the hill waiting for opportunities for things to change from the difficult climb to the easy ride. But we all know that nothing in this life is easy and devoid of consequence.

In the 3rd chapter of Lamentations, the writer expressly speaks of the hard walk everyone on this earth experiences by exampling his days of struggling to climb back up the hill. There is not a moment in time in which we cannot understand that the actions we take in our youth will eventually come back on us and bite us in the proverbial behind.

We all desire to have good lives. We all seek out those people who can assist us in making the climb into the box more enjoyable and easier than the last go-round. But somehow the more we seek an advantage in getting ahead, the steeper the path becomes.

Then things go out of control and we end up falling outside of the protection of that box we once enjoyed. Those who rode with us, well, they disappear and we are left in a place which seem to offer aid or light in any portion of the situations we are overcome by.

By the time we get through verses 4, we can see that the examples of stress, hurt and the days of being alone in the struggle are more than real in the life of the writer, but also in the things we are / have faced. There seems to be no answer to the prayers thrown up to Heaven. And the calls to family and friend seem to be blocked by God solely for the intent of making our hearts bleed. And when those some timey friends do call, all they do talk about is how bad we look and how hard we have fallen. What great friends huh?

If we consider the movements of those children on that hill, we can see that their actions are free-spirited and filled with a trust that they cannot utter. This is the moment we recall that the Lord is never far from those that trust in Him and will openly call upon Him for salvation from the circumstance which is causing all the heartache and grief we are experiencing

Once we have stopped rolling on the hill. We stand up and begin running to the bottom for another opportunity to climb back to the top. But this time, this time we have a better view of the challenges offered in the walk up and we take more assured strides because this time we are not leaning on our friends, but on the ONE who not allow our feet to be moved (Proverbs 3:5–6).

> Read Lamentation 3:1–26

Make this day the day you decide that the journey you take is given to the Lord in prayer so all things you consider to do will be blessed and cover by His Hand of mercy and grace.

CONSIDER THIS ON THIS DAY

busy roads

SOME OF THE STRESSES which we deal with daily, seem to be exclusively designed to make us feel as if the world we created is crumbling. In the middle of all that, we begin to think that the problem experienced is only happening to us.

But the moment we meet up with people and begin to discuss certain issues, we discover a sometimes-elusive fact; we are not alone in suffering hard trials and situations.

In I Corinthians 10, the writer opens the doors on our ignorance and sheds light on the saving grace of Christ Jesus and His ability to structure situation ending avenues of escape.

We are never left alone to fail, but shaken enough that we reach out to the community of Believers for support and prayer. If, if we remain attached to the community of Believers long enough; our stumbling and our falling will not occur quite so often.

If we remain in the community, we will be reminded that there is strength in numbers.

Read I Corinthians 10:12–13

Make this day the day you put your focus on the only one who can lift you from your storms. Remember you are not in this life alone. There are people who understand and can empathize with your struggles and will pray with and walk with you.

You are not alone.

CONSIDER THIS ON THIS DAY

who are you before God

If we would step back & take a moment and look at how we act in the presence of God and in the testimony, we try to live; we fall short every time.

Those things that have been accomplished in our lives—we somehow take the credit & proceed to add another feather in our caps and puff up our little chests as if we are the best slice of bacon on the plate.

We still fall short.

In the 8th Psalm, the writer doesn't mince words when he has the realization that those things concerning the universe and all of creation, God chose us to care for the most.

After all the times that God has been placed in our little "holy boxes" and opened only when there is trouble or when we are on program; we fall short.

Pride causes us to miss out on a great deal of blessings and bountiful grace, because our thoughts are not on Him and what He has and can do in our lives, but how much greater we can MAKE OURSELVES; we fall short.

Take a moment and think on all those times that that one day should've been your last day. BUT GOD was mindful of you (us) and carried you (us) over.

Read Psalm 8

---

and realize that He is with you every second of everyday, so open that little box and allow Him to make you great in ways the world can only see His light shining through your testimony.

CONSIDER THIS ON THIS DAY

an everyday friend

THE APPROACH WE HAVE toward those who are in our circle of influence and those people we only associate with at work, school and during our daily grind is greatly influenced by our attitude, how we are feeling and then our desires to learn more of the world to better ourselves.

But there are those people who seriously believe that the few things they've experienced in life, the books they've Read, lectures they have sat through and the changed views of history given by the media will give credence when have social interactions with someone who is not of their common circle.

We all have varied lives and personal / cultural history which overrides those things offered in history books, the History Channel and profound lectures given by highly decorated teachers. Let's face it, history has written by the victor and all other accounts have been either watered down or totally dismissed as not being truthful. Those accounts giving by our grandparents and those senior people in our lives give details which will not be found on the internet or in any classroom.

No one knows your story; nor can anyone dictate how and what life has taught you.

In Proverbs 18, Solomon details the changes which are required for anyone who has a desire to become greater in the relationship they have with God and then with those who come in and out of their daily walk in this life. The first thing Solomon starts with is the position the person has themselves at the beginning of each day—separated and in prayer seeking the wisdom of God. One issue that keeps arising in our days is the fact that we do not separate ourselves from everyone long enough to hear from God or meditate on those things learned.

The value of a friend far outweighs all the "head knowledge" one can obtain, but learning of the friend from "heart knowledge" allows for those barriers to be broken and trust built in its place.

In verses 4–9, Solomon lists out the reasons why anger and hate grows and friendships end. The end is based in wrongly gathered information, words spoken out of turn and the selfish need to always be right and correct over the respect of the other person. Then there is verse 10 repeating the need to carry out the steps listed in verse one. If we could only put God first in all our actions, the majority of our dealings with people on a daily basis will become less stressful.

It is the approach that we use in our dealings with those in our circles of influence that are suspect and requiring the greatest changes. Verses 20–24 we can Read the words Solomon wrote with fervor and see that love outside of ourselves is a necessity when trying to cultivate and maintain good relationships. To be a friend, one must listen intently and then speak honestly.

Questions can arise from Solomon's mentioning the value of the wife and the blessings afforded the man who has his wife as his friend. The answer is simple and direct. If a man can interact with his wife on an equal plan, respect her conversation and ideas; then he will be able to openly accept, hear from and then listen to his friends outside his home.

The acceptance of another person's story should take precedence. They and their pangs should matter above any preconceived notions or learned formula.

The friction develops within most relationships because there is a great deal of talking and not a lot of listening. For this relationship to become fruitful, both parties must be open (at all times) to listen to learn the issues of the heart and not listen to only to respond because they are in a conversation. The latter does not a great deal of thinking, but the action of loose lips; thus, the friendship sinks.

Read Proverbs 18

Make this day the day you choose to remove yourself to that quiet place and make request of God to be bestow wisdom where all your knowledge has failed to provide the bridges needed to maintain good Christ-centered relationships.

CONSIDER THIS ON THIS DAY
true emotional payback

THE POLICE HANDCUFFED SANDY and put her in the car

Neighbors watched as her live-in boyfriend was carried away in the ambulance

Several mentioned how much they screamed and fought

Others spoke on how she would have to walk to work or catch the bus in the rain

Only a few said that he was a good man trying to make a life for them and how he kept his car clean and was always at home at night

None saw the failure in the many times he was seen slapping her before she walked away to work

Everybody was stunned to learn that she had somehow glued his hands and arms to his body

Two officers were heard saying that they had grown tired of coming to the house for domestic violence calls and that he got his just paycheck

Not a true story

But why should any one person put up with not being treated as the queen she should be just to have a warm body in the bed?

There should be a moment of thought in any relationship when realization comes and facts do not fit. No one is someone else's property—> especially if the couple is not married.

Why work hard at work and at home and not receive any benefits of becoming better in the midst of your struggle?

Realize this—what you put into a negative relationship will result in receiving certain things in return; most not worthy of you are what and who you were created to be. Your dreams should be paramount to the person who says they are in love with you. They should never seek to place themselves or anyone else before you

In 2 Corinthians 6:14, it states that those who are not compatible in spirit and in nature should not dwell together in unity. The question from the text asks, "How can someone who has been blessed with talent and gifts settle for another who has not one good thing to offer in the positive in any relationship?"

Let us face the facts; some people deserve to be alone . . . no matter how good they look, what job they have, the size of the house they own or how much money they can carry at any one time. If all of this does not line up and add up into growing you to become a bettered person ------ walk away.

The answer lies in the following food for thought:

CAN see yourself living in your current state for 5 or 10 years and being happy and fussing and fighting and arguing and not having any money to meet bills nor take your children to the places that will allow them to look toward grabbing a good future for themselves?

Is a bad and negative relationship worth 10 years of undue pain and strife?

If you had to stop and think Leave that paycheck and walk away

---
Read 2 Corinthians 6

Make this day the day you decide to truly love some people with a long-handled spoon.

CONSIDER THIS ON THIS DAY

who am I to receive such grace?

IF FOR ONE MOMENT, one minute in our day, if we consider all the things we have chosen to do that are outside the standards of being a good Christian, all the times we strayed from the boundaries which our parents have set, how could we then call ourselves good Christians?

Is the calling based on His grace?

Then we fail to understand that grace isn't given for continued acceptance of poor and useless choices so our fleshly desires can be fulfilled and satisfied. Those things are temporary and cause great difficulty after seeing how much has been lost for the sake of a moment's satisfaction.

Sanctification is defined as the process in which the believer is being made holy by separating them from their bad choices, poor decisions and the sin which will cause a difficult fellowship between the believer and God.

In Judges 16, we see that Sampson has played the full gambit of being a fool; all the while knowing the boundaries of his parents, the life of a Nazarene and the standards in which God had laid out for his life. Yet, he still lived as if the grace of God would remain continuous as he plunged deeper in acknowledging God's purpose for his life.

Justification is defined as the active process of declaring or making something righteous in the sight of God.

Becoming a follower of Christ is not an instantaneous process in which we lose all our inhibitions and become so holy that we walk away from those desires and dreams which are not fulfilling in the purposes for our days here on earth. Our purpose is to be open and accepting of those things God is and has removed from our lives as we come to a better knowledge of who He is and the reasons why Jesus sacrificed Himself for people who would become complacent in their fellowship because of grace

Can we continually take His grace for granted and expect to be a blessing to family and friend and then fulfill our purposes before we die?

Read Judges 16

Make this day the day you look back and see how far God has brought you from and realize that the journey remains a continual learning process toward justifying and sanctifying a better life for your children, grandchildren and those who are always watching your Christian walk.

CONSIDER THIS ON THIS DAY

talk is cheap and does not need repeating

THE PROBLEM WITH DIRT . . . MOST would think that if they would talk about a person or bring up their past repeatedly, it would cause harm, tear up your day, stop you from moving away from them, end the pointless relationship, break you down, force you to quit and give up and make you stumble back into the old you . . .

BUT there is one thing to understand about dirt . . . the more it is tilled, turned over, cultivated, pruned of trash and debris, broken apart and a loosened; the better air and water can get to the through. It is those tough things that that we all must go through, which teaches us lessons and strengthens our resolve and relationship with God when and while no one else wants to hear our pleas and tears.

God sees our tears and knows what we should become . . . despite our past . . .

Most and all who know of our past does not take the time to speak good things into our days, but they tend to look into the negative and feel that somehow those negative days and bad decisions have rule over our lives and throughout our days—causing us tough times.

It is those tough times which allow us to drop a tear, and then realize that those friends who use our failures and faults to prop themselves up to be better people than us can be just like a leaf on a pear tree in the winter time—gone for good. Let them talk themselves out of a good friendship.

Think on this:

When one is working in a garden, the first thing which must be done; it the breaking up of old ground and rocks and soil. This is what Jesus does in our lives when we ask for certain blessings and gifts . . . our days and lives must be prepared for the seeds of good fruit to be planted.

In the book of Isa. 28:24, the question is asked—Does the plowman plow all day to sow? Does he open and break the clods of his ground? The problem with the Plowman is that he has no concern of what comes behind him. He is just there to break up the old stuff. There is not a thought to what is to become of the tilled and turned over dirt.

But is the Plowman and our friends and friend-enemies would realize—is that the more they turn over and till our dirt, the better we become in this world.

We serve an awesome God.

We serve a God that keeps giving us—chance after chance after change after change after chance after chance after chance . . . and before you know it . . . we are not the same person that we once were. We somehow have a better understanding of the 3rd chapter of the book of James

We somehow can just shake off the dust and dirt thrown at us by the people who are supposed to love and care for us

How can a man (or woman) speak of love to you and call you names and use words he would not use to his own dog? And you love him back?

Start believing in your own talents and stop waiting for validation from a "selfish fool."

We somehow can look back at the fields of our lives and truly say, "how did this happen and how did I get over?"

So, on this day . . . take this scripture with you . . .

"Sow to yourselves in righteousness, reap in mercy; break up your fallow ground: for it is time to seek the LORD, till he come and rain righteousness upon you."

Let them talk . . . Let them talk . . . Let them talk . . . Let them talk . . . Let them break up the ground that you are unable to look at or talk about . . . BUT when they do . . . speak the Word over your life . . . Speak positive and great things into the days of your children, your spouse, your brothers and your sisters . . . Speak over yourself and wait for the God of another chance to make the great changes in your life . . . Let them talk and point fingers . . . Let them stay busy looking at piles of dirt—While you walk on with the blessings of good fruit.

It is He that will come behind the Plowman and adds increase into fields that are said to be bitter, useless and barren. God has made us to be the head and not the tail . . . stop accepting everything people say about you as if it were the Gospel . . . Speak over yourself those things that you have prayed into your life . . . Speak great things into your days . . . stop repeating what they have said about you as if it were true . . . Speak great things into your days because God did not make you to be anyone's footstool or mat.

You are a Child of the King . . . So, act like royalty . . . Speak like the royal you truly are.

Speak the Word over your house, over your car, over your job, over your children and in all your days!!!

Reference Scriptures:, Romans 8:1–14, Isaiah 28:24–24, Philippians 4:13, Psalms 103:8–13, Hosea 4:1–10

CONSIDER THIS ON THIS DAY

going at it alone

BUT THERE ARE THOSE people who know us, walk with us, cry with us and get angry at the same things we do. These are the people that we enjoy having around. These are the people that inspire us to do better and reach for higher goals.

If the choice has been made to follow Christ and all the examples He has left, then GOOD friends are attribute that should be acquired and cherished. In Matthew 8, he speaks of the fellowship of GOOD friends being a benefit when all know Christ and are open to make request based on the need of the friend, the pain of a loved one and the need of the family and church and the whole time directing all things to God and not dishing out dirt on any subject. These actions allow you to see the power of God within His children and then in yourself.

United Prayer is the catalyst that will change habits, behaviors and the foundation of personal faith. Good company does not corrupt good morals, it strengthens them.

Yes, the Word does make it known that the devil is like a lion . . . seeking who he can destroy. The Word does not tell us that the devil is seeking a group of people, but that one person that will try to do things on their own and out of the strength of the fellowship. Yeah, I paraphrased . . . but there are only certain instances that individual success can be achieved and that success is only for that person. But when there is success by a group, it not only grows the power of the group . . . it makes all around stand up and take notice and then join into the group—adding strength to the group.

I do know that we have friends and associates that are known from childhood. At some point in time, the idea of a childhood friend should be dropped because we no longer are dealing with child-like issues. The enemy would like us ignorant and looking backwards. There is no growth in the future if the only thing thought about is recess, playgrounds, 8th grade dances, old high school loves and things left in the halls of a school you never return to.

This makes you distracted.

This makes you a target.

The devil may at times attack, but his attack fails when each person in the group remembers WHO is in the center of the group and WHO is the power source that allows the group to move as one. It is the familial draw of the group which gives singular focus to the problem and the solution.

Sometimes.

Sometimes.

Friends from the past that offer no positive incentive in your future MUST be left to be exactly what they are PAST FRIENDS. It is time for you to link up with stronger people to acquire and obtain those things God has gifted to you and your family . . . old friends can say hello to you at the class reunion and then you can tell them how good God has been to you

Make this the day that you open up and trust God to put GOOD people in your days that will inspire, encourage and push you to reach your full potential.

CONSIDER THIS ON THIS DAY

not for you

Looking at the past two and three months, the amount of distress, stresses and upheaval that society constantly is throwing in to our daily grind, some may lose hope and not seek a time of solace.

Finding relief for those things which cause us to have pause seems to be a new enigma, clouded by a world of grief, anger and frustration.

The only option, sometimes, it to head to church and seek an answer from the Lord; yet the outlying message we receive from some church folk is that those things from God are for a certain and select few. So, then our last nerves seemed to become a little more pinched and our hopes for relief in the one building that is supposed to be the refuge during all storms, has caught us some hellish storms itself.

In the Gospels of Matthew and Mark, the same story is given of a woman stressed to her limits and at her wits end. Out of her concern for her daughter, she stepped outside of her normal circles and cried out for help. But while Reading about her actions, we come to realize that even the Disciples of Christ had thoughts that all the things taking place had something to do with them, when they uttered these words, "She cries after us."

The craziest thing to learn in this Christian walk is that there are some people who think that the movements of God in the lives of His Children, have something to do with them and the positions / titles they have acquired. The Disciples didn't ask Jesus to send her away; they demanded that she be sent away.

When we look upon the actions of the last few weeks of some church folk, who call themselves Christian and then listen to them descry who will receive and when Christ Jesus will move in the lives of believers and non-believers, it seems as if they are caught up in the same moment of emotions as the Disciples were.

This walk is not for a specific people. No one can say, "This is not for you."

To call upon Jesus is that of a personal matter. A relationship which cannot be dictated by no one on this earth; no matter their degree, pedigree, bank account, years of service in the church nor the color of their skin. NO ONE HAS THE LOCK ON THE ACTIONS OF CHRIST JESUS.

If we can take a moment and walk back the days of our lives and consider all the changes we have been taken through and survived, we can then realize at some point we tuned out the deniers and naysayers and went to Christ on our own to receive those things needed to heal and get us back on our feet. (Heb. 4:16)

Read Matt 15:21–28 and Mark 7:24–30

Make this the day that you decided to stop listening to the media and all the outside sources during your storm and go directly to Jesus to gather up all the crumbs of blessings bestowed you.

CONSIDER THIS ON THIS DAY
do you really need convincing?

M<small>ANY HOURS OF THE</small> week are spent asking ourselves questions about the "HOWs" and "WHYs" which are based in us looking toward the future with hope and keeping a faithful aggression on the things we know God will do if we just, "hang on a little while longer."

Most of our daily issues fall upon us so quickly that we lose sight of those items we have prayed on and the directions God has alReady spoken into our lives. The craziest thing is that those who are in our inner circle fail to stand with us when the storms arise and the challenges come to shake the foundations of our faith. They ask questions as if they don't know who we are or why we choose to stand strong in the knowledge that Christ Jesus will not only keep us, bless us, but He will ensure that His Promise to be with us is fulfilled.

Exampled in the 9th chapter of John, the writer details the actions of Jesus over those remarks made by His disciples when they questioned the origins of physical failure in one man's life. Is it not strange that Jesus had to keep making the point that all things done in this life are for the glorification of God?

The story is simple and straightforward. A person is caught up within a storm, never makes a request to Jesus that he be given sight, but all those things which have been burdening him all his life are removed because someone outside of this man's circle of influence invited Jesus to take a look.

All the hours within our daily grind are not so heavy that we cannot look around and ask Jesus to step into the lives of those we know and personally do not know. From the person who speeds passed us on the freeway at ungodly speeds to the unfriendly store clerk who may be living through weeks and months of not seeing the light at the end of the tunnel. We should be able to take that abounding grace, which is overflowing in our lives, and ask Jesus to reach out and comfort them and give them the peace and joy we have gained by keeping our heads down and understanding that failure only comes when we quit (Phil 4:13).

If we can walk back the days of our lives, we can see all the changes God has permitted to fall our way and those blessings that have been granted. Still we can voice that we have been asked by others, "how we got over?" and "when did you change?" These are those visible cues which allow God to get the glory from others marking our walk in Christ, because we don't move in the same circles, talk the same way and we somehow keep looking for higher ground in the Lord to better ourselves.

With all the things that we have struggled through, today we can realize that those struggles have only increased our faith and made us stronger.

Should not the strong reach out to ensure the weak are not left behind?

> take 4 1/2 mins and Read John 9:1–41

CONSIDER THIS ON THIS DAY

been there; done that

Struggles, strains in life, stresses throughout the work and school day and then you arrive home to a whole new set of problems.

The bottom falls out of your life: You lose your job, can't make all the monthly bills and still have food on the table, the love of your life cheats and leaves, the car breaks down and then the cat died on the front porch.

Seems like a never-ending cycle, right? Working hard and then harder, paying attention to every single detail in life to make others happy and ecstatic about the possibilities of living a totally blessed week and month.

Things change. New job comes through and you're making more money than before, the stress levels are lower and that nagging, daily headache has left and then you have met someone new and all the birds are singing praises of a new and loving relationship for you. This change took some effort, some work, some heart-healing desires and a great deal of praying and biting your tongue.

You've made it!!

In the 4th chapter of the book of Philippians, the Apostle Paul makes specific references to two women and the issues that they are experiencing and that the same problems they are dealing with, are some issues everyone must face at some point in their lives. His reference to them wasn't to put them on notice or as a show piece in front of the church. His calling them and the church out to work together and solve the issues facing them because it would do some harm to the church. Paul had a desire to move the focus of these people from the problem, to the Problem Solver.

Have you not considered that those issues and problems we deal with daily have an indirect effect on the people who are around us (the church in particular)? It is how we address those dark days and how we seek to handle those issues which shine the light on our physical health and our demeanor. In other words, it is how we look to other folks when we are going through some things, which cause them to take pause and question our Christian walk.

The Apostle Paul makes a direct appeal to the church and these women to look to those things that they have learned and received from him through his actions, teachings and watched him do each time he visited their church. Several times in this chapter, there is a push for the church to openly trust God and then lean on one another in honesty, truth and through prayer.

Life is alReady hard. We cannot do this thing alone and be successful. The church, no church or community can be successful without Christ and without a praying church community. If one part of the body hurts, we all hurt, right?

Struggles, strains, stresses and heartache happen. But when we take it to Christ daily the hope of success is greater than the burden of failure and the desire to give up and quit. We have all bottomed out at some point in the days we have been here on this earth. The strength we have and always seek comes through Christ, good praying friends and family and the joy which comes from the peace of God after we gotten up from our knees and left that large party of crying and stressing over things that ONLY HE CAN CHANGE.

> Read Philippians 4:1–14

Make this day the day you choose to trust God, call those people you have not talked to in a while and let them know that the things they are struggling with are life ending. There is PEACE IN CHRIST JESUS and all things can be overcome with you praying with and for them. This Christian Journey is not all about us, but how we spread the Gospel of Christ through our actions.

CONSIDER THIS ON THIS DAY
this and that

MANY OF THE CONVERSATIONS we have with the people in our daily grind contain a great deal of us trying to explain ourselves, the reasons behind the drive that is within us and detail information as to why we smile when things around us seem to be falling apart.

It is most difficult to explain the testimony of faith that we live under and in to those who simply refuse to believe that they cannot control or change every facet of daily life. And this is the reason that we choose to see the empty cross of Christ as motivation.

For many, the image of a man pinned to a cross is reason for thanks and allows them the motivation to make it through certain circumstances. But that is only half of the Gospel message. The completion of Christ's work took place early one morning and has fallen into the laps of those who choose to believe that the cross and grave are empty, and choose to see that their testimonies are displayed in the lives that they live.

In the first chapter of I Corinthians, Paul delivers the best message a believer can give to a hurting world. In this chapter, Paul gives definition of his history, who he is and has become due to the empty cross of Christ and why he is continually delivering the message of Good News to a church of young believers. In his explanation, Paul tries to explain that there is no defined logic in who God reaches in HIS efforts to offer salvation through the testimony of those who can see through the simplification of the message and actions of Christ and the reasons that there is hope when on looks upon an empty cross and grave.

In many of the conversations we have through the week, many seem to continually point to this situation and that circumstance, but never see that God has the undefined power to change lives, minds and hearts. The barriers that are in place are in place because so many people truly believe that they can outsmart God and out-maneuver all the tides that come from the daily storms we all face from time to time.

Here is the shocker in all of this, there is no image of Christ that can be more hopeful / helpful to the believer and to those who are seeking direction and an end to their never ending, self-inflicted struggles.

Some look for a sign and others seek higher heights through education to gain a better insight of who Christ is, was and will be in the lives of the believer. Those actions are limiting when all things of God are based in the relationship we have with HIM and the testimony we deliver to all those people who question our walk and hate on us for all the blessings we receive as the result of coming to a better knowledge of Christ (Matt 6:33).

Read I Corinthians 1:1–30

Make this day the day you choose to let your testimony and light shine openly to all who watch and then speak to you. There is no reason to ever be ashamed of the saving grace of such a great God.

CONSIDER THIS ON THIS DAY

check the optional box

Being kind and gentle to the people we pass on the street can often become difficult because of non-responses to a good morning or opening a door for a stranger, who is carrying a few packages. Yet, a man being chivalrous nowadays will be taking as "hitting on a woman", so most guys don't open doors for women they do not know. This is based on personal reflections and my choices to continue opening doors for others, whether they say thank you or not.

What is stuck in the cycle of "why keep doing anything nice, loving or charitable to others" is the simple-minded attitudes which make one check their stance in Christ and seek to increase the personal ability to bite one's tongue and not say something out of the way that will ruin a good mood.

When Jesus was asked, 'what is the first commandment of all?' His answer wasn't shocking. It was the immediate follow up that He offered which contained conditions that most folks have issues with.

In Mark 12, Jesus was being confronted by people who had question based on and bordering on selfish intentions. Sometimes we are in a place to that our moral character is questioned, not on what we know, how deep we believe in ourselves and exactly where God resides in our lives. The person who asked Jesus the question, alReady knew the answer to his question. What he was seeking was validation in the action of not having to deal with others on the same level as a person should deal with God in their daily grind.

The issues of not wanting to say good morning to people we don't know seems selfish, but society tells us not to speak to people we truly don't know. But we all work in places where co-workers can pass one another in the hallways, parking lots and stand in elevators and never say a good or kind word. Yet, we choose to call ourselves to be in the image and sect of Christ Jesus.

While having a difficult time during any portion of the day, we seek to check the optional box when it comes to being loving or even acting like we are of a friendly nature. And then there are some who are just are mean for no reason at all and spend the greater portions of their day complaining about any and everything. Somehow they've check the optional box and then returned to draw a circle around it.

Being gentle and kind hearted in today's society is seen as weakness. Yet those who call themselves strong and independent are those same people who say they love Christ, but build boundaries in such deep ways, that the most loving of people possesses strong issues working with or lending a helping hand to aid them.

But then there is the examples and love of God that calls us and the pushes some to reach outside the box and show a little love.

Read Mark 12: 25–31

CONSIDER THIS ON THIS DAY

the swing back

Confrontations in our days will occur. It is how we respond in those instances that shows our true nature and maturity.

After one has experienced failure and heartbreak on a deep level, the thought of over reacting in heated conversations lessens, and the ability to listen to what the other person is really saying takes over. We remain silent because in most heated discussions, those things we hid seem to get a life of their own and begins eviscerate our character, personality and destroy the testimony we have been trying to build.

Sometimes it is not what we say, but how we deliver the anger that has been welling up inside of us for this particular moment. And yet, it feels so good to blow off some steam, scream and shout and then let a few curse words fly. But then we ask the question, was it really worth acting out in such a manner to destroy another person and then our light we claim to have as a Christian?

In Ephesians 4, the Apostle Paul begins the chapter talking about the job we have to do as Christians. He gives detailed directions on how to walk bravely in an ignorant and mean world. He tells us what characteristics we should bolster and then how to model our lives after the example of Christ by letting some things die off each day that we can rise and be renewed. The scriptures which garner the most attention are verses 26 and 27.

In thinking over those lines, I often think of Jackie Robinson and how he demonstrated the best of his God-given talents, not through anger, but through his swing back at those who'd seek to destroy his character based on their own limited abilities and selfish hearts.

THE SWING BACK

Yes, it is in the way we deliver our response in confrontations which can either make or break our day. The best choice is to come prepared, having the best characteristics of a Christ-minded person on hand. That is; take at least two seconds before responding and then do it with a smile, while aiming for the fences.

It does take some practice to get through and then overlook the petty frustrations and arguments within a day. But you will be better off not engaging some folks and then realizing the all conversations directed at you are not worthy of your time. Especially if the sole intentions of the other person are to draw you out of who you've become and back into that old person. You are better than that.

Read Ephesians 4

Make this day the day you choose not to be engaged by the petty and cruel, but walk in the light as you are called.

CONSIDER THIS ON THIS DAY

loving all day long

THERE IS ALWAYS A level of misconception when it comes to the depths of love, charity and then caring for someone outside of the family circle. The limitations are based in blood and locale and not familiarity.

The idea of loving someone outside of our families, must reside in our having the audacity to love in the examples of Christ Jesus; without fail. Which means we keep our hearts on our sleeves and love all with the greatest strengths we can muster.

In the 13th chapter of Corinthians, Paul gives the best definition of love being a life's behavior and not a simple action verb. Though there are those who would take this chapter and work it to squeeze tithes and offerings out of parishioners and congregations through the guilting of them somehow not caring for the church unless their money is coughed up and then some of the blessings of God will be bestowed into their days.

Carrying out particular tasks which tax our behaviors to grow is an uphill fight. Especially when our lives are surrounding by images, billboards and words from our circle of influence telling and warning us to "take care of self above all others" and still see ourselves as the model of Christ.

The Apostle's words to the Corinthian church and to us, displays the need to not have barriers, attitudes and expectations; which come in the way of our Christian walk becoming like his.

To love like Christ Jesus did (all day) is having the desire to make the "good" choices, based on the spiritual standards HE spoke of when HE said, "love your neighbor as yourself." Now, that right there is a difficult task for the Christian of today. All things concerning our neighbor has been politicized, quarantined and spun into a realm of hate which only the media and Satan can truly enjoy, because it keeps the distractions at a feverish boil and the church distracted from hearing a word from God.

Read I Corinthians 13:1–13

Make this day the day you call that one person you've not spoken to in months and give a solid word of encouragement.

CONSIDER THIS ON THIS DAY

think before acting

Most of our days seem to steep & endless, uphill climbs.

The ability to counter this is with planning, preparation and good advice; which centers on the people we allow to feed into our lives.

Proverbs 24 gives us directions on how to be wise in our choices of friends, associates and enemies and when to listen to each of them.

It is nothing like falling on your face and have the same people who gave the advice to you, ridicule you behind your back.

This is where active wisdom comes into play. USE all the knowledge you have gained so far & then bring it all to God in prayer—sifting through all the advice and desires you have to be successful.

Yeah, you may fall. But you will get up again and again and again.

YOU ARE NOT A QUITTER !!!

Read Proverbs 24:1–16

Make this day the you trust in your ability to climb your mountains alone and with God's Hand guiding you.

CONSIDER THIS ON THIS DAY

walking blind

NOWHERE IN LIFE ARE we guaranteed anything. Ours is a life based on "blind faith" and the trust that we put into believing that when we fall asleep, we will awake in eight hours or the food we purchase of the store will sustain us and not kill us—graveyard dead.

Hebrews 11 issues direct insight into the reasons why we live in the definition of faith everyday & take it for granted . . . evidence.

There is evidence all over creation which points to God's Hands being active in every second of our everyday. So why can we not openly trust Him to lead us through the storms we face?

Read Hebrews chapter 11

Make this day the day that you open up your mouth and tell God you trust Him to take control of your life and lead you toward becoming the person He created you to be.

CONSIDER THIS ON THIS DAY

done right, family is important

Many of us have had those weeks and months which our dealings with family & in-law was detrimental toward our attending family functions and church services, we couldn't breathe. It has gotten so disgustingly bad; some do not attend either function.

The base problem in that one decision—we forget why we are supposed to pray for and love on one another. So, we let days and years pass by, while the family deteriorates and no fellowship can be restored. THE RELATIONSHIP REMAINS—no one can stop being a brother or sister or uncle or mother in law. The fellowship is that active catalyst which allows spiritual bonding to become the direct flow into bringing the community of family back in line to God's blessings.

In the book of Ezra, the writer details the Children of Israel returning home from being captive and broken after decades of long and bad decisions which caused the community of family reason to falter and fail.

It takes time to heal. It takes guts to reach out and make requests of family (blood & in-law) to fellowship as a complete unit. The one thing that we all forget in the divisions of family is the children's not having access to familial live, support and history.

It should be our duties to bring the community of family back in line with those things God has bestowed on and in each family. Bringing family back together with the STRONG intent of regrouping and fellowshipping in His House first, will allow those old hurts to heal

---

Read Ezra chapters 1–3

Make this day THAT day you put all things in God's Hands and move to heal all the broken heartedness which is distracting you from hearing from Him.

CONSIDER THIS ON THIS DAY

problems with roots

A GREAT DEAL OF our failures & successes occurs because of the circle of influence we have acting in our daily grind. Our "friends" can either be the reasons we keep suffering losses or the purpose for our fallen to our knees in tears.

We allow others to dictate how we feel & believe about ourselves.

From our birth, God has placed within us great and grand purpose backed with remarkable talent. On the inside, we move easily and with power. On the outside, we let SIMPLE MINDED folks manipulate our belief in ourselves. We allow others to crush our self-esteem.

In Judges 16, the story of a misguided young man is given to us as examples of how our friends, lovers and enemies find ways to remove us from the gifts and standards God has placed within our walks in life. Samson had serious faults and problems which caused him a slow stumble to defeat, solitude and failure. He allowed others to distract him from the CALLING WHICH GOD HAD GRANTED in his life. The root of his problem was that he believed the talents and gifts were only to please his wanton lusts.

If, only for a few moments of the day, if we take a step back and check ourselves against what we know and understand about God . . . we could correct our missteps.

Correcting our missed opportunities takes some hard work, it takes some pleading and praying to God for forgiveness, and it takes US making the decision to break away from negative and non- prosperous friendships.

Samson had to completely lose everything to understand his missteps and find himself being treated like an animal, working hard and receiving only ridicule and laughter from the very persons he may have thought admired him because of the talents he possessed.

Read Judges 16:19–30

Make this day the day that you make time to investigate the issues which are causing you to suffer and struggle needlessly. Then systematically MAKE STRONG DECISIONS TO REMOVE INFECTED ROOTS AND CAUSES so you can restore you to you.

BELIEVE IN ALL OF YOUR GIFTS & TALENTS GOD HAS GIVEN YOU.

You are greater than folks have been telling you.

CONSIDER THIS ON THIS DAY

going through some things?

Facing daily challenges may be a tough pill to swallow and maintaining a smile in the middle of the pressures is laughable.

Nothing in life is easy. Not falling in love, not landing that great job and career, not trusting friend and family with any amount of money and then wanting to be a strong Christian on top of those things, one could almost quit and throw in the towel and have the world eat us up.

But we walk in the hope that all the things we have seen and learned of Christ and saw how it wasn't by our power that we didn't have to survived the last storm alone . . . it was our hope in Him and wrapped with just enough patience to wait for the battle to end in our favor. We survived and conquered one more challenge and knocked down a few more obstacles.

In Romans 8, the writer tells us that we are not alone in dealing with life's challenges, addictions and frustrations. He gives us direct examples of the promises of God to never leave us alone and that the presence of His Spirit in our days, will grant us those opportunities to be and become conquerors on a daily basis. Yeah, overcoming small trials is a victory. Don't sell yourself short nor think that God will not be with you through ALL THINGS FACED while you are going through some things.

You are greater than the storms you will face. Believe in yourself and Believe in the God who has created you to be a great person

---

Read Romans 8:24–37

make this day that one day you decided to not only stand up and WALK INTO YOUR STORM, but trust God to deliver all the power, strength and direction needed to get your victories and control of your purpose.

You are MORE THAN A CONQUEROR in Christ Jesus.

CONSIDER THIS ON THIS DAY

wasting time

THERE ARE CERTAIN EXPECTATIONS people have of us and our talents and we have a greater sense of who we are and what we are willing to do. In short, the expectations we choose to match our character and personalities are sometimes more complex.

Not one person can tell you what your net worth is to those who love you and depend upon all your actions and decisions until the personal decision is made to put and keep God in the forefront.

The pursuits of becoming a productive & profitable adult and viable Christian is based on desires and choices.

We must make daily choices to walk upright and blameless. And many times, hold our tongues because there are several colorful words which would emphasis our exact emotions and destroy the antagonist trying to breakdown the person we have become.

In Acts 1, we find out that Jesus has taken His journey home and left instructions with good people who have a steep desire to be seen as right and high standing in God's eyes.

The call goes out for a person to replace Judas Iscariot's vacant position in the brotherhood. Out of 120 men & women in the room, two are picked because of the way they carry themselves in and out of common view.

Life is way too short to pitch pennies against the wall. God has granted us a few years to get things right and leave good impressions in those who come after us. Judas dropped the ball several times. His replacement was prepared and alReady practicing to be better because the man they were following. In short, he put himself on the back burner to meet the expectations needed to be known as the person he desired to be and the one God calls all of us to become.

> Read Acts 1:12-end of the chapter.

Make this day you choose to take the higher calling of Christ in your life.

CONSIDER THIS ON THIS DAY

you heard me

THE EXPLANATIONS OF LIFE are not hard to distinguish after God has spanked our hands, given instructions on where we should go and how we should live to fully understand the reasons why He blesses us the way He does.

In our hardheaded walk in this world, we continually ignore the boundaries God has set up for us and the lighted paths He places at our feet. We choose to go varying routes because we see hills and mountains in the paths He has placed in front of us.

Acts 2 shows us that God can and will knock down as many barriers as He can to get our attention. He used the 120 men and women to introduce the Holy Spirit to the world and offer invitations to all for the sake of soul saving.

The path God placed in front of us has some difficult miles, kilometers and depths. These are part of the journey. They are a part of the cardio workout we need to have our hearts, faith and minds strong enough to handle the changes the enemy will throw at us. But again, we fail because we choose to try our own maps, as if travel the same beaten paths, the destination will have a different ending.

Read Acts 2:1–37

Make this day the day you stop talking and listen to the Holy Spirit speaking to your heart.

CONSIDER THIS ON THIS DAY

getting off our high horse

It seems the older we get and the more we learn, we tend to take a great many things for granted. We move in and out of our busy days as if we control all the blessings which come our way. We forget that all things begin and end with Jesus' grace.

We walk passed people without any type of "hello or good morning" as if Christian Love is only for the people we know & fellowship & worship alongside of as "members of the body of Christ"

what rotten members we truly are!!

In Philippians 2, the writer gives distinct reminders to the church, that no individual in church should feel that they are above reproach because of title, financial status or by the manner in which they feel "blessed and highly favored." The writer states that WE all should have the same mindset and that our thought patterns should resemble that of Jesus'.

Does scripture tell us that Jesus walked passed folks and didn't offer love?

Then why do people who regularly attend church and say that they are a part of His Family?

Paul wrote this letter to let the church at Philippi know that the good work they were doing could be destroyed by having sorry and selfish attitudes.

Read Philippians 2:1–15

CONSIDER THIS ON THIS DAY

Make this the day you choose to be more like Christ and spread some love through a good greeting or head nod. It won't kill you. It may just wake up the love in one other person who is struggling to see the good in this day.

CONSIDER THIS ON THIS DAY

waiting on fear

As we wake each day, we do it we a small excitement and expectations to see new things takes place. None of us truly like to wake up and think on the impending problems which may or may not arise during the daily grind. But we take steps into the fray, knowing God was there before we woke.

In Psalm 27, David lists out the reasons why we should not have a friend in FEAR. He goes on to tell us that all our confidence and trust should rest in the Hands of the Lord.

Mike Tyson once spoke on his facing fear as being the catalyst which pushed him to win boxing matches and believe in the talents he honed to perfection.

How do you face your daily fears?

In verse 6, David gets happy and shouts when he realizes that those he feared the most could not overtake and destroy Him once he rested on his trust in God.

Read Psalm 27

Make this day the day you throw caution aside and step strongly to God and ask Him to lead you in greater directions to conquer all your struggles.

CONSIDER THIS ON THIS DAY

ruts, ruins and being ridiculous

Let's face it, God has given everyone on this planet a good sense of right & wrong and the understanding to either get things to survive or gain wisdom to be fruitful and sustained.

But there are those who refuse to use better judgment because of the fear which rides along with taking the FIRST STEPS toward becoming a productive / responsible adult. They would rather sit and live in the cycle of "barely making it" and "blaming everyone else." These are those people who have no desire to accept God's plans and purpose for their lives and will give up on trying because they have fallen short of reaching long term goals once or twice. SO THEY SETTLE FOR THE MUNDANE.

It takes growing up to be a productive / prosperous adult and we all know some ADULT CHILDREN who refuse to break the cycles of being needy, messy and negative

In Exodus 14, shows the examples of what God will do for His Children and to those who sit in the way of His Children moving toward their blessings. In the middle all our storms, God sheds light on the path He has for each of us, but the problem which arises is that we GET IN OUR OWN WAY.

In the pursuit of dreams and goals, the decisions made in the heat of the moment can either allow us to sit on our hands and cry because bad choices are shown to be ridiculous after we watch others pack up and move on to better days.

THAT IS THE TIME TO STAND UP AND WALK OUT OF THE RUINS of failure and unbelief.

> Read Exodus 14:11–18

Make this that day you finally get tired of not having and not doing enough to reach your dreams!!!

CONSIDER THIS ON THIS DAY

stuck up & missing out

If we would step back & take a moment and look at how we act in the presence of God and in the testimony we try to live; we fall short every time.

Those things that have been accomplished in our lives—we somehow take the credit & proceed to add another feather in our caps and puff up our little chests as if we are the best slice of bacon on the plate.

We still fall short.

In the 8th Psalm, the writer doesn't mince words when he has the realization that those things concerning the universe and all of creation, God chose us to care for the most.

After all the times that God has been placed in our little "holy boxes" and opened only when there is trouble or when we are on program; we fall short.

Pride causes us to miss out on a great deal of blessings and bountiful grace, because our thoughts are not on Him and what He has and can do in our lives, but how much greater we can MAKE OURSELVES; we fall short.

Take a moment and think on all those times that that one day should've been your last day. BUT GOD was mindful of you (us) and carried you (us) over.

Read Psalm 8

And realize that He is with you every second of everyday, so open up that little box and allow Him to make you great in ways the world can only see His light shining through your testimony.

Have a great & Christ-centered day.

CONSIDER THIS ON THIS DAY
shut down but still able & willing

Yeah.

Yeah.

Life throws a bucket of mess at us daily. Sometimes it feels like 10 are thrown at the same time and from odd directions, like friends and family, who smile and go on as if they are supposed to challenge our salvation and hope in God.

BUT GOD gives us so much more to hang onto and hope in that shutting us down for a moment ONLY INCREASES THE REASON FOR A DEFIANT TESTIMONY.

In the 4th Chapter of Acts, we find that Peter, John and the 40-year-old man, who was lame have been locked up for a night and threatened with their lives if they spoke of THIS JESUS AND THE SALVATION HE OFFERS. The strongest examples come when each man opens up to the Spirit of God and refuses to stay silent in the midst of others not wanting, for the second time in two days, to hear or accept the Gospel of Christ Jesus.

What does it say about you to others if they not only see Christ in your daily walk, but hear your testimony in all the victories you face each week?

So, I say to you on this day—choose the best weapon you have in your life and allow the Holy Spirit to add into your every step through every waking day so you can shake some hardness out of the lives of those hating on you and trying to shut you and your family down

---

Read Acts 4:1–31

---

make this day the day you drop chains and speak great things into your life.

TUESDAY

The Flow Hasn't Set In Yet

CONSIDER THIS ON THIS DAY

a point of no return

ANOTHER YEAR HAS CROSSED the half-done mark, and some of us are in the same pit we were in at the start of the year and carried over from three years prior. Still filling the pit in with diminished hopes and dashed dreams.

What is the cause of this yearly cycle?

In Ezekiel 22, God is talking to the prophet about the problem of discipline, focus, respect and reverence. The same issues we have in many families these days. Ezekiel is given a tour of the history of the families he has been giving the Word of God and those God has been watching. He (God) then asks several times, where are the men who should love Me and direct their children toward Me?

Disappointment comes when we realize that God is not pleased in the actions or inaction His children take in not raising strong and determined children.

He is looking for KINGDOM MEN AND WOMEN.

This world is eating up our children and for some reason, the church has decided to deliver & accept mediocrity. We allow negative and lazy people to dictate away the directions of God for limited successes and borrowed hopes.

The quality of lives of our children should be paramount. Our lives in front of God should be better than the people who came before us.

The problem is NO ONE WANTS TO BE HELD ACCOUNTABLE. So our children suffer. And they suffer greatly, because they don't know God like they should because our testimonies just don't line up on any level.

CONSIDER THIS ON THIS DAY

Read Ezekiel 22:1–31

Take a minute—one minute—to sit down and ask God where you are not meeting His standard causing you to remain in the same negative cycles month after month. Then ask Him to create your days so you can raise up all your family based in successes wrapped in His Grace.

CONSIDER THIS ON THIS DAY

hold your head up

As a Christian, I have come to realize that no situation can cause me to lose the grace and power which comes from having Jesus in all my days. I do understand that every day is a battle for my sanity and salvation, but through Christ Jesus I shall remain a constant conqueror.

Read Romans 8:35–39

CONSIDER THIS ON THIS DAY

captivated by your stance

THESE ARE THE DAYS when all that you do is on display and scrutinized for flaws.

These are the days that you must think before you utter the wrong words into someone else's hearing and upset them because they will either cry that you are judging them or that you feel you are better than they are.

These are those days spoken about in Ezekiel 22, where God takes the Prophet and asks the question, "where are all the people who should stand in the gap and prove to the world that there is a greater standard to live by?"

This is that day you choose to make all your days a living testimony for the Lord.

This is the day you not only speak Kingdom things into those who are scrutinizing your walk, but captivate them by allowing the Holy Spirit to dictate your responses.

Read Ezekiel 22:1–31

Let them watch & talk, but you choose to walk the path God has destined for you. They can either catch up & walk with you now or look for your footprints later.

Be the Kingdom Child God called you to be.

CONSIDER THIS ON THIS DAY

success is a step from heartache

AS A CHRISTIAN, THE path I am walking in this life should be so well defined that those who know me take pause and consider the reasons why I AM FOLLOWING JESUS then take similar paths without trying to make me deviate from the direction HE HAS CHOSEN IN MY LIFE.

I am on a path to become greater in this life and be the example which causes my friends to see the positive glory and grace God offers daily.

Read Romans 8:27–32

Success is just a step away.

CONSIDER THIS ON THIS DAY

you know it alReady

I CAN SAY TO a fact that we have all had discussions with people who truly think that they know it all. They have memorized a few scriptures; the back ends of several sermons and can even regurgitate someone else's prayer as if all of it was from their heart.

The moment the attitude is taken, "I alReady know this", is the moment the movement of the Holy Spirit is stifled in the life of the believer. It is the moment self-righteousness begins to grow and the Word of God loses its attractiveness.

We become Puffed Up.

In I Corinthians 3, Paul admonishes the church to realize that the believer must diligently seek the best of and deepest mysteries of the Word. The other side of his conversation to the church was that they stop acting like children because the little knowledge acquired in the first few years of meeting Christ IS NOT THE END OF KNOWING HIM.

We live in a cynical world, which is Ready to devour the stagnant and proud Christian.

In this week's journey, take the time to LISTEN TO OTHERS SPEAK THE WORD and find out if you know it all or can be filled with a deeper desire to learn more of Christ. Because the moment you settle, is that exact moment the enemy starts eating at you and your family.

Read: I Corinthians 3:1–16

CONSIDER THIS ON THIS DAY
the ability to walk on water

AS A CHRISTIAN, I may have several days a year where I am quiet, seem distant and lost in thought or even moody.

Those are those times that my soul is in preparation for impending storms & trials. My lack of speech & staring off is me praying through the bad days before they set foot in my present.

prayer + preparation + trusting in Jesus = walking on water

This is the ability to rise up and walk on the water of the word and travel over and through your situations and circumstances.

CONSIDER THIS ON THIS DAY

self-serving worship

SOME OF OUR DAYS are filled with a desire to get ahead, succeed and find someone to love for a lifetime, but those things take work. And in this society, who has time to give-give-give, when the joy is being on the receiving end?

God commands us to be fruitful and multiply, right?

Most of us take that to only mean, GET MARRIED and have children. But the start of being fruitful means that each person MUST DO THE WORK REQUIRED PRIOR TO RECEIVING prosperous bounties.

In II Chronicles 7, there was an 8-day worship service after the Temple of God had been built and after Solomon had taken an entire day praying and preparing God's people for worship. The story shows us that as soon as we leave church, the realization of the worship service isn't about God, but the items He places in our days for us to achieve and succeed.

But still God remains waiting for His children to be open and honest in worship at church & at home. II Chronicles 7:14 isn't a rally cry, but directions and information toward all of God's children becoming fruitful and multiplying & spreading the truth to others and bringing them into the church and increasing the family of God.

Read II Chronicles 7:1–16

Make this day the day you choose create more positives in your days which prepares you for your impending blessings.

CONSIDER THIS ON THIS DAY

AS A CHRISTIAN, MY testimony should remain the catalyst which causes me remove myself from negative situations, unsavory places & parties and walk away from anyone who would openly work to destroy my fellowship with Christ and ruin my reputation.

There is a difference between good friends & Christian friends.

CONSIDER THIS ON THIS DAY

who's I am

WE LIVE IN A fast paced and cynical world. If you don't automatically fit in and are accepted by the larger crowds; one can feel shunned. So, we work at being like the world (stuck, selfish, hateful & full of pride).

God called us to be and become peculiar people. Those individuals who stick out in a crowd and have a better grasp on this life than others can ever imagine.

In Genesis 1, God created man and woman to be just as He is . . . a Constant Gardener. We are to take care of and tend to those items in our lives that He has blessed us with. That means how we act & how we display ourselves to the world should be above those things which satisfy the world.

We are who He has gifted us to be. A proud people, determined to show off the fruit of our labors. Not because we have done anything better, but because He has granted us opportunity to tend in His garden and rule over the short life we have here on this Earth. We are made in His image. People should see Him in all our actions, right?

Read Genesis 1:25–29

Make this day the day you choose to be and better with the blessings you have been given & stand out in the crowd because you cannot remain following the lead of this world.

CONSIDER THIS ON THIS DAY

sometimes silence is not golden

There are those moments in a relationship when one partner should stand up and help or correct the other. But issues arise because one person refuses to hear from or trust the words of the person they supposedly love and arguments ensue.

This cycle is repeated so often that neither partner offers up words of wisdom or advice, but rather stands back and watch their lover fall on their face and ultimately hurt the relationship & family.

My question to those in that type of relationship is, "why are you wasting your time and theirs if you constantly refuse to partner up, work together and speak up?

In Genesis 3, we have been told constantly that it was Eve's fault for the fall in the garden, but if you would look at the scriptures, you will quickly realize that her "man" was standing right there and silent.

Life and relationship are too valuable to stand in silence and watch love, family and dreams crash and burn. It is far better to say what is needed than to suffer both spiritually & physically when unneeded storms arise from inaction.

Take this journey serious and handle up on all you should do to shore up yourself & your partner / spouse so you can continue to hear from God

> Read Genesis 3:1–9

Make this day the day you say something positive in your partner's / spouse' day.

CONSIDER THIS ON THIS DAY

AS A CHRISTIAN, MY attitude is that one thing which can either draw people into church or allow them to see Jesus.

Or my attitude can be that singularity which keeps people from believing at all.

A responsible person finds a way to remain humble & kind

CONSIDER THIS ON THIS DAY

the reason for fear

NOT ONE DAY PASSES where we do not take steps to avoid concentrating on our bills, family issues and broken relationships.

We want and desire long days filled with peace and time to breathe. The only way this can be accomplished is by focusing all our resources to flow to and from God.

We want to avoid as much stressors as we can. So we don't mention the people who irk us, the bills that frustrate and won't go away or the distant future which looks like our yesterdays.

Psalm 27 is written by David as instructions on moving in faith and trust. Though most of the problems we face lead us into uncharted waters, we must realize that the God we serve create the elements which join together to sing praises to God in the open spaces of Earth's waterfalls.

Read Psalm 27

Make this day the day you open up and trust and shout through your dark days because God will see you when you first step into it and remain with you after you step into *SONshine*

This is the day you trust God for your increase and step into it

CONSIDER THIS ON THIS DAY

accepting all deterrents

Reference Scriptures: Proverbs 1:1–9 & 4:1–12

HERE WE ARE IN a world where the bold Christian is scared to live and speak the word of God, because someone may be offended, either by the actions, the beliefs or the just hearing the word and having it invade their souls.

Here we are in a world where being politically correct is supposed to be the norm, but that changes the moment one person screams that they feel violated by a belief system they say is outdated.

In basic terms, these folks are fearful to live to a higher standard.

The term to fear the Lord simply means to live in dRead and awe of His total being. This causes the believer to have a desire to become more and more like the Lord is.

What the Christian should realize is that we serve a God who is omnipresent, omniscient and all powerful. He is not a fairy tale that can be wished away because some say that they refuse to believe in a God they cannot see or hear from. That is their choice. Our choice is to live in respect for all that He can do and that He will do in the lives of all creation; whether they believe in Him or not.

In Proverbs 1 & 4, Solomon makes the claim of how to approach and then live in fellowship with God, with an open mind and a child-like heart. It is in that approach the Christian should take the correct steps in learning of and hearing from God as if it is the beginning and we are learning things

ACCEPTING ALL DETERRENTS

all over for the first time. But that takes discipline and this world is so far removed from a disciplined life that it is almost laughable.

Here we are in a world that does not take God seriously, but wants the blessings of God to be there because they can eat, breathe and work. Every creature on the planet can do that. The difference between the believer and the non-believer is the believer tends to take on more of God's character and walks in less fear of the world.

For you to get passed the point you find yourself today, is to begin to realize that you have nothing to be fearful of and all things to gain. The world will tell you that your socio-economic status limits where you can and cannot go. The word of God tells you that you are more than a conqueror and that you can do all things any time of the day and any hour and in any minute that you decide to put feet to the faith that you claim you possess.

CONSIDER THIS ON THIS DAY

AS A CHRISTIAN, WHEN looking at all the blessings in my life and all the trials I have overcome with Christ on my side, GIVING UP & QUITTING IS NOT AN OPTION.

> Read Psalm 23

CONSIDER THIS ON THIS DAY

being prepared

Let's face it, there are thousands of ways to obtain and gather the needed information to better our lives and the futures of our children, but most of us would rather sit back and take in the things others tell us, as if their words are fact.

"there is no better fool, than a lazy fool."

Week in to week out, we wait on others to give to and feed into our lives without the thought that there are those folks who live to destroy the dreams and hopes of others. But it is at our disposal to reach for a better understanding in all things and not settle for mediocre teachings because it made us feel good during a 30-minute sermon.

In II Timothy 2, Paul is speaking to each individual in hopes of building a stronger community in and out of church by telling them that they (we) need to be prepared to SIFT through ALL THINGS PEOPLE TALK ABOUT AND TO US; our futures are always at stake.

Let's face it, the smarter cell phones become, the lazier the user become. We still wait until someone else does the research and tells us what they think we should know.

Since we are caught up in so many storms in life, why wait for someone else to tell you how to avoid being hit by lightning?

Read II Timothy 2:15

CONSIDER THIS ON THIS DAY

making it all right

AS A CHRISTIAN, MAKING promises to God and keeping them should be as valuable to the Christian as air is to the lungs.

He holds up His end AND ANSWERS PRAYERS... silence comes in the Christian's inaction of not following through.

playing church hurts the entire family after flaking out on promises and commitments made through prayer

---
Read Phil 4:13

Be about God's business all day

CONSIDER THIS ON THIS DAY

be about it

AS A CHRISTIAN, THE purpose that God has placed in my life for me to fulfill does not require validation from any man, woman or part-time evangelists.

What is required in the walk of the Christian is a strong fellowship with Christ Jesus in the middle of their living testimonies being aligned and on full display, so others can understand how the Gospel changes the lowest into the greatest

---
Read Matthew 28:19–20

Be about God's business all day

CONSIDER THIS ON THIS DAY

who are you and how are you standing?

As we move forward on the actions of the Holy Spirit, we fall back into the mindset of the Believer and the choices that are made during our daily grind. Attitude plays a great deal into the status of our lives and the depth of the blessings received in the upcoming weeks, months and years.

Assertiveness—the ability to express feelings, beliefs and thoughts and to defend one's rights and beliefs in a NON-destructive manner.

Positive assertiveness is based in the foundational growth of EMOTIONAL INTELLIGENCE, which offers a balance in that is needed to convey all that s on that individual's heart and mind.

In Romans 12 (entire chapter) Paul is speaking of the gifts that the Believer has been blessed with by God and has been cultivated by the Holy Spirit. Each office should be handled by individuals who can carry themselves in and out of the daily grind without losing or damaging their character in their administering of their gifts in the offices they hold.

Character—distinct mental and moral qualities which can be equated to an individual

The Six Pillars of Character—Trustworthiness, Respect, Responsibility, Fairness, Caring, Citizenship.

In the Robert Burns poem—we can see that he was in line with all the items Paul discussed about the "good" man moving his community forward in the middle of growing his family and his character (name)

Read Romans 12

Is There Honest Poverty—Robert Burns (http://superforest.org/2009/12/robert-burns-a-mans-a-man-for-a-that/)

QUESTION:

What does having a "good" name mean in being a Believer?

What sets or drives a Believer to seek a "right" life?

CONSIDER THIS ON THIS DAY

planted

AS A CHRISTIAN, MY being committed to a person, a relationship, an organization, or thinking on a plan of action means all areas and all facets of each step toward success is taken to God in prayer before steps are taken, words are spoken and before promises are broken.

Because if I did all things under my own assumptions and judgments; things would end up falling apart.

Read Psalm 1

CONSIDER THIS ON THIS DAY

correction is better than failure

SOMEONE ONCE SAID, MISTAKES happen. They never clarified the beginning or the end of the MISTAKE. Just that it has taken place. No one mentions the consequences or the fall out. Just, MISTAKES HAPPEN.

poor decisions or improper planning must be the root cause and not one person can say, I AM RESPONSIBLE.

Taking ownership of failures and mistakes is the first part of maturation (physical, emotional & spiritual).

The writer of Psalm 39 gives credence to the reasons the Believer of Christ should be and become a strong example of God being active in all areas of life.

Taking ownership within the relationship strengthens the boundaries of trust and admiration. It is not the open opportunity to be ridiculed or laughed at, but that teaching moment where the Believer regroups and repents AND moves on with a better understanding in getting closer to God and completing certain goals, covered by His Grace.

Sometimes the chastisement hurts, but we get up a little stronger and more determined not to repeat the same things with a lackluster outcome.

NO ONE LIKES TO FAIL.

Read Psalm 39

Make this day the day that you trust God for direction, reproof and restoration. Not one person can ascend to higher heights alone.

CONSIDER THIS ON THIS DAY

created to become greater

It seems as if our purpose in life is to work hard & make major decision after major decision. This is where planning, listening and praying comes into play. We all have certain dreams and desired goals that we would like to accomplish before our time here runs out, right?

Stop settling for mediocrity and living repeated cycles that have the same outcome. It is HIGH TIME TO CHANGE YOUR CIRCLE OF INFLUENCE if no one in the circle has changed the way of thinking or addressed the issues plaguing the entire existence.

Time should be set aside where we can make plans in silent and then think back on all the advice which we failed to recognize as legitimate. Yeah, most of us hate to receive direction and instruction; we have our own brains to think, right? But the failure in that framework is that WE DO NOT KNOW EVERYTHING.

In Hebrews 12, the writer is giving the basis of how to receive instruction in the middle of being frustrated and burned out . . . look at those who reach out to you and those who fed into your becoming who you are as an adult. Then take the examples of Jesus and press onto the goals God has set for you. It is not hard. It just takes you getting out of your own way.

Read Hebrews 12:1–15

Make this day that one day you decided to make the change needed to get ahead and reach your dreams.

Openly tell God that you are Ready and able to hear from Him & follow His guidance. Then watch how much stronger you will become

CONSIDER THIS ON THIS DAY

experience and wisdom are great gifts

TRIPPING AND FALLING IN this life is not easy or acceptable. No one likes to be surprised by things breaking down after months and weeks of planning.

Sometimes we need the guidance of those older than us and sometimes, the people we know who have had the misfortune of having a lot of success and losing, only to regroup and begin their run at life anew.

Not all advice is gravy. But there are always morsels of information that we should sift through to Readjust our walk so we do not trip and fall after having made request of God to show us the directions to move.

In Philippians 3:15–17, Paul gives the church the best directions for sustaining church fellowship and a strong walk through this harsh world. He suggests that each Believer locate and befriend those who are focused on similar goals in Christ and learn of them as examples on how to see life through a Christ-centered focus.

Take all advice with a grain of salt. Sift it through your experiences and in your daily prayers to see what is right and wrong. Your future rests on how sure footed you become on your pursuits of desired goals and dreams.

Allow no one to sway you from the purpose and calling God had placed in you—stumble but keep moving using what you know to regain your balance. And the things you do not know, reach out and asked for help & direction. A little wisdom goes a long way.

CONSIDER THIS ON THIS DAY

when life gets hard

There are those days where all the storms we have faced and walked away from seem to recycle on that singular day and smack us in the gut and forces us to fall on our knees

The problems associated with falling on our knees are heavily based in our inability of letting all things go the moment we call upon God

In John 16:33, Jesus sums up and entire sermon with four words, "in me is peace." The hardest thing for the Believer to grasp is peace; because they want to hold onto the hell that has risen in their lives as if they can repair, remove and destroy things because they open their mouths and scream empty phrases like, I DECLARE & DECREE without giving over to God or changing the bad behavior of putting themselves first

Jesus tells us in this chapter that as long as we are living, we are going to face hard times and issue . . . but . . . we can have hope in Him because He has dealt sufficiently with this world.

Read John 16:33

Make this day the day you tell God you trust Him to direct your days and then give it over to Him.

CONSIDER THIS ON THIS DAY

tragedy is not a game ender

Noticing that eyes are always watching you, is not a notification of increased haters. It is a sign that you must have something in you that they want to immolate. I am not saying that you are the best, but you have obtained certain qualities and standards that have been blessed enough, that folks around you would like to either acquire or duplicate.

Either way, the stay in ear-shot of all your actions, whether they are positive or negative. THEY WANT TO SEE YOU SINK OR SWIM. And most likely, all they see is you swim out of the storm with God's assistance. Don't frustrate onlookers with harsh n bad words, educate them on how they should open up and meet God when their life is falling apart and they must make decisions to either sink or swim.

In the book of Ruth, there was a decision offered amid several storms. Ruth chose to stay with Naomi, not because Ruth was holy, righteous or blessed. She chose to stay because she saw something holding Naomi up after her husband died, left her alone in a country of strangers and with no prospects.

The thing that was in Naomi, caused her to refocus and move toward her faith in God.

Sometimes, it is not the amount of times we have failed, faltered and come up short which brings people to want to watch us. It is how many times we continually call on the Lord and how we respond in the storms while He moves us to a sure-footed area. They watch and watch to see how strong the testimony is before they begin to regurgitate our actions and words into their lives.

Tragedy does not mean that life is over and we should quit. Taken in simple doses, tragedies can be the catalyst which seals our testimonies in Christ and opens the door of salvation to those who have not experienced Him removing the weights of their burdens, baggage and broken hearts.

Read Ruth 1:1–17

Make this day the day that you choose to be a Naomi or a Ruth. Both attitudes are life changers and soul savers. The blessing comes the second you choose to STAND UP IN YOUR FAITH and move toward Christ with full strides.

You are greater than your situations and circumstances.

CONSIDER THIS ON THIS DAY

problems and pains can be a catalyst

SOME OF THE EVENTS in our lives can be equated to having someone punch us in the gut. The sudden loss of job, the heartbreak associated with a relationship ending, and the passing of a loved one. All of these can be those things which should cause us to self-evaluate and seek God for a corrective plan while we navigate our future based on the changes that caused us to fall on our knees.

In Psalm 40, the writer details his hurts and pains. In the middle of Reading the Psalm, we fail to realize that the writer states that while he was down on his face, God met him in the same position.

All through our weeks and months of struggle, God keeps His promise to always be with us. As David wrote in Psalm 23, "His goodness and mercy shall follow . . . " If His goodness and mercy are following, that means the Lord is right there with us.

YOU are never alone in this journey.

Read Psalm 40

Make this day the day you accept the Lord's help in getting you out of your storm. Why try to conquer mountains on your own, when you have help each step of the way?

CONSIDER THIS ON THIS DAY

stuck is not going anywhere

Does it not seem kind of strange when we run into people who are educated and talented, yet they are still living a mediocre life and do not have the drive to do anything within their talents and gifts?

We heard it time and time again, the only thing which holds an individual from achieving and obtaining is that on little thing that rests within them. No matter how much encouragement given, they seem to bask in the glory of not doing so they won't be called a failure.

Is that the one thing holding you back, someone calling you a failure?

In the first chapter of Joshua, we discover that Moses had died and the children of Israel were without a leader for the first time in 40 years. Not only did they not have a leader, their access to God was cut short. But God had made provision in the case something did happen to Moses. He had created the man of Joshua—attitude and all. He was chosen by God.

God had a conversation with Joshua in the first nine verses of this chapter and gave him all the tools he would require to take all that was promised to the children of Israel. After having repeated the promises that He had told to Moses, God filled Joshua's ears with them again and then added, "Be of good courage." What is it that hinders and retards our flow forward in life, even after we have prayed and cried and then God answers?

Ours is a cynical life. We ask for things then we refuse to take the steps or make an effort to achieve the littlest of successes because of fear someone will see us leaving their circle of influence or stuck in the pattern that if God blesses us, we must wait on family to make the decision to follow us as we follow God's call in our days.

Look at it this way, Psalm 115:16 tell us that all things on this Earth were created by God for human consumption, protection and control. But failure arises because the lack of courage and the ability to believe in self.

The time has come for us to make the decision to either believe in God and His promises or to walk away and accept being a quitter. Courage is that animal that will force you to run straight ahead and only question your steps once you have reached your goals. If you have prayed and thought over certain paths of action, what is causing you to drag you knuckles in pursuit of what God has granted in your life?

If God has promised it, where is the failure originating.

CONSIDER THIS ON THIS DAY

why are you different?

TRANSITIONS, CHALLENGES AND TOUGH times faces each person walking this Earth. The question arises which asks, "WHY ARE YOU ALWAYS GOING THROUGH IT?"

Some people fall apart and cannot function as soon as they lose a job, lose a lover and confidant, or a broken relationship finally goes flat. But then there is the person of YOU. Situations shake you, but have never completely broke you down because you find your solace in prayer and determination in asking God for a little more strength. And when He answers . . . it is relaxing to know you have not been abandoned.

In I Peter 2, the Apostle writes very candidly about the way in which the believer is to move in this world and remain in fellowship with God. He revisits the joy of the first time we all met God and understood how quickly His grace moves in our lives as if we have bitten into the sweetest oranges on the planet.

The change in the letter comes when he (Peter) challenges us to become and remain different in a world seeking to be mediocre and similar.

You are different because you have accepted Christ into your life and you have this understanding of how great you could become IF YOU CHOOSE TO LEAVE NEGATIVE THINGS BEHIND. Leaving negative things means you are always smiling, always seeing the rainbow during the storm, not cursing folks out because they refuse to TRUST IN GOD AND NOT THE PAYCHECK at the end of the week.

You have been chosen to be different because you refuse to settle on anything less than the best. You have been chosen to be different because some of your friends refuse to hear from God, but will see Him in you—THE MOMENT YOU CHOOSE TO BE SET APART by God.

You are different because you have sat in Bible Study and Sunday Service and desired more than the "rope performances" that go on each week.

You have been chosen because you have tasted the goodness of God and the little morsels given on Sunday are matching up to the world and you realize that being in Christ is much, much more fulfilling.

Those who are falling apart because of little storms and negative relationships need to see a different light. They need to see the real person you are becoming and not the one you pretend to be . . . because you think you can hide this Christian thing to fit in with them.

Is it not time for you to stand up and walk away from the children's table?

Read 1 Peter 2:1–15

Being a Christian is not easy, especially when you decide to be different in your pursuits.

Make this day the day you choose to become the person God has created you to be . . . let your light shine so all who know you can ask how you got over and you can show them JESUS IN YOUR LIFE because you are eating at the grown up's table.

CONSIDER THIS ON THIS DAY

stop crying—drop the kleneex & get back on your feet

Facing daily challenges may be a tough pill to swallow and maintaining a smile in the middle of the pressures is laughable.

It is time for you to take a deep breath, stand up and realize that the little setback DID NOT KILL YOU, IT JUST MAD YOU MAD ENOUGH TO GATHER YOUR TALENTS & STRENGHTS.

Nothing in life is easy. Not falling in love, not landing that great job and career, not trusting friend and family with any amount of money and then wanting to be a strong Christian on top of those things, one could almost quit and throw in the towel and have the world eat us up.

But we walk in the hope that all the things we have seen and learned of Christ and saw how it wasn't by our power that we didn't have to survived the last storm alone . . . it was our hope in Him and wrapped with just enough patience to wait for the battle to end in our favor. We survived and conquered one more challenge and knocked down a few more obstacles.

In Romans 8, the writer tells us that we are not alone in dealing with life's challenges, addictions and frustrations. He gives us direct examples of the promises of God to never leave us alone and that the presence of His Spirit in our days, will grant us those opportunities to be and become conquerors on a daily basis. Yeah, overcoming small trials is a victory. Don't sell yourself short nor think that God will not be with you through ALL THINGS FACED while you are going through some things.

You are greater than the storms you will face. Believe in yourself and Believe in the God who has created you to be a great person .

> Read Romans 8:24–37

Make this day that one day you decided to not only stand up and WALK INTO YOUR STORM, but trust God to deliver all the power, strength and direction needed to get your victories and control of your purpose.

You are MORE THAN A CONQUEROR in Christ Jesus.

CONSIDER THIS ON THIS DAY

change is required

Most of us talk about wanting to be better and do better and do it with great passion. We pray and pray and pray. And frustration comes when things do not go our way. We tend to raise fist at God and try to move mountains on our own. Bad choice.

Failures arise because there is that one moment when the decision is required to make changes in behavior, lifestyle and the circles of influence we have become accustomed. The decision forces us to rethink all the information given to us over a lifetime of experiences, which pushes us to have seen Jesus as more than a man who died on a cross. We are forced to open eye and realize that He is one portion of the Trinity and our access to God and His amazing love for us.

In John 3, the writer details a conversation about change and what that change offers the Believer. Most don't get it or just refuse to understand that being a Believer of Christ Jesus is an internal and constant happening. The conversation deepens when Jesus makes it known that all who hear the offer of change will not accept something which is quite simple and open. This is where the lifetime of knowledge holds many back. They refuse to let go of old ideas and Earthly based knowledge and trust in the Eternal Change which grows both the information and directions in this life to a greater and better development of the individual.

Read John 3:1–20

CHANGE IS REQUIRED

Make this day the day you step back and realize the Jesus we keep wanting to pin to a cross, is much more than the image. He is God and He can / will do anything for you if you move toward His standards of worship and living.

CONSIDER THIS ON THIS DAY

say it and say it loud

It's not hard to get information these days. One has the options of cell phone, tablet, laptop or desktop. But most times those items are used to look up and spread foolishness, untruths and items which will fuel anger in many others who accept all things on the internet as being truthful.

It only takes a minute to do a little snooping, right?

II Timothy 2:15 tells us to be mindful of all the things learned, heard and accepted. And then Paul takes a step further and warns us about the fallacies of being embarrassed by not knowing and then delivering useless information.

In Psalm 89, David writes of examples on the delivery of the information and how it should be done in joy, with full knowledge of where the source of the information is, how it makes you, you and who it is that should be the filter for your life through the daily grind.

Read Psalm 89

Make this day the day you begin to Read into all the things you accept into your life. Do a few minutes of research and then bounce it off the things God has caused in your life.

Then you will have FAIR AND BALANCED news.

WEDNESDAY

Take a deep breath, waterfalls ahead

CONSIDER THIS ON THIS DAY

blessed assurance

IN THE MIDDLE OF most of our weeks, we experience some type of brewing storm and pushback from a coworker, family member or friend where there should be none.

Strange huh?

The week and month can start off with a bang and we feel overly confident and overly blessed as we walk cheerfully through the month. Then comes that day that is the middle of our work week, where someone throws a wrench into the works. Though they try, we seem to fold up inside and find that place that we can regain strength, focus and the solace of the Lord which resides within each of us.

In Psalm 91, the writer details the reasons why the believer should understand the assurances God offers on a day to day basis. Changes will come at us in varying degrees, but as the writer opens this text it becomes apparent that there will be nothing on this earth that will hurt us in a manner that would take us from the presence and safety of God's Hands.

Sometimes the middle of the work week can be difficult and challenging and then most frustrating. But the moment we desire to throw up our hands and quit, the Spirit of the Lord steps in and calms our emotions and clears up the storms building within us.

So, after you've Read all of this, take to heart that those days of frustration only last for a moment, but the joy of the Lord is with you far longer than you can imagine.

Read Psalm 91

CONSIDER THIS ON THIS DAY

Make this day the day you choose to let go and let God as you trust in Him a little bit more.

CONSIDER THIS ON THIS DAY

who is watching your actions

AS A CHRISTIAN, I realize that am the sum / total of each adult who impacted my life as child.

It is up to me now to make positive decisions b/c a child is watching me today.

> Read James chapter 3

The image we give to them today, effects their tomorrow.

CONSIDER THIS ON THIS DAY

concerned about what

Each of the past 10 days you have either come to a complete stop in your pursuits of becoming a greater person and stronger Christian because of one simple distraction OR you have taken pause to reconsider your walk with Christ and how much time you should give to HIM in your day.

You cannot afford to walk in this life alone, nor can you handle the onslaught of changes which travel in each storm you face. You need a partner, friend and confidant who will not leave you for a nano or atto-second.

In Psalm 23, David puts before the church, his reasons why he can have blessed assurance through all the challenges to his life, his throne, to his children and then to his relationship with God. This is the reason he could stand in front of the children of Israel after writing this and say with a believing voice, THE LORD IS MY SHEPHERD . . . . .

It takes confidence inside of your faith, not only to speak your beliefs, but WALK IN YOUR FAITH through all of the mud which follows the storms. Yeah, you have to get your feet muddy in this walk. If you didn't your stance in later challenges wouldn't be so steadfast and unmovable.

Read Psalm 23

Make this day, the day you begin to trust the Shepherd who has never abandoned one of HIS sheep.

CONSIDER THIS ON THIS DAY

a praise break????

SOMETIMES WE GET LOST in the translations and cannot see God through all the changes people take us through or hear from Him because a few of the church members are doing more talking than listening. We have all been there. We hear a familiar scripture and then tone out the messenger, because we know it all and forget the reason behind the delivery of the sermon.

Understanding and learning takes the effort of being open to new & old ideas. None of us of computer driven. We forget & we overlook.

In Psalm 89, David takes the time to reason within himself all the actions God has upon the life of the believer and how consistent His love and mercy is toward hardheaded people. We want what we want and we do the things that please us first.

The reason behind the praise break is to stop, think and remember all the moments in life that there were times we should have been rendered mute and buried. BUT HIS GRACE IS MORE THAN SUFFICIENT when it comes to us, the hardheaded and work driven people.

The reason behind the praise breaks are to give God His praise and remember just how much He has changed our way of living.

Read Psalm 89

Make this day the day you raise your hand and tell God—THANK YOU . . . THANK YOU . . . THANK YOU for the things HE HAS DONE and will do.

CONSIDER THIS ON THIS DAY

move on & live

Life is hard enough without some folks working daily to remind you of your failures, falters, bad choices and old sin-filled life. These are the same people you wonder about if they are ever going to grow up or come to a better knowledge of what the process of Salvation really is.

Romans 8:1–14 sheds light on the issues a Believer must deal with, the flesh & the spirit. In the flesh—the Believer has to deal with Earthly desires & the enemies of God. In the Spirit, one must deal with the issues of giving up and allowing the Holy Spirit to lead, guide and give daily protections.

These are a constant battle. Then we must deal with decisions on who to trust, God or the friend we have grown up with and have allowed to become our mind of reason, when they are in the same negative cycle.

How can we take advice from people who have no power or control on the rising & setting of the Sun? Why do we listen to the so intensely? How many times have you been praying and God shouts into your soul, "you are sorry & worthless"?

You do the math.

Who has failed you more, friends or Christ Jesus & who can offer you "better" days if you call and open up and fully give your trust?

make this day the day you decide to move on from your past and trust in God for the increase?

CONSIDER THIS ON THIS DAY

Stepping lightly is a mistake

THERE IS NOT A day in our lives that we should tip toe around the storms we face. As a believer in Christ, we should have the wherewithal to look at each circumstance we have got to face & each situation we have caused and immediately turn to God for answers & directions.

Having faith is one thing we can repeatedly say. But HAVING FEAR IS BELIEVING IN THE ENEMY and believing you are a failure before ever trying.

In Psalm 37, David tries to reassure believers that fear is a waste of time when one waits, trusts and then listens to God speak into their days.

WHAT POWER DOES FEAR GIVE TO SHAKEN OF HEART?

David sings out this Psalm, not from a position of guessing, but of having experienced the full favor of God when he looked through his own storms and saw God's answer on the other side.

Read Psalm 37

Make this day that day you throw caution to the wind and stepped into God's favor & grace.

CONSIDER THIS ON THIS DAY

a place of my own

AT THE BEGINNING OF each day, most of us take pause to think on and prepare for the trials which follow the sunrise. That pause that we consistently take is that moment we breathe in and ask God to take care of us.

None of us try to take the blessings of God for granted, but we do tend to get comfortable in the realization that HE is always with us.

In Psalm 40, David found a place in his life for God. It is the place where we all retreat when the storms of the day work to overtake and destroy all the strength we have. But if we would consider giving God a place in our walk, that is not just at home, but a space that He can talk to us before we start the car, turn on the computer at work, wake the kids up for school—we would see that as soon as we open our hearts to hear from HIM, HE is alReady moving to comfort and protect us in our daily grind.

Read Psalm 40

And understand that when get done with talking to God for that brief moment, HE will add a new song into our souls. Victory is yours to have. All you have to do is start your day with a little talk.

CONSIDER THIS ON THIS DAY
taken for granted

Facing all of ups and downs life constantly throws at us by way of our children, friends, brothers and sisters, and spouses causes us to tremble in our walk with God.

In Ephesians 2, Paul reminds us that God gives gifts to His children on an unlimited basis, but we tend to take Him for granted on a larger scale, while we think all our actions are truly acceptable.

We treat people like dirt and then greedily expect God to be the constant rewarder.

Something must be given in our daily walk. And the giving must come from our side of the relationship. We must trust Him and be faithful to Him and only Him in the same manner as He is with us.

All the ups and downs cannot shake us from His love . . . all we can say then in those circumstances is . . . BUT GOD.

BUT GOD is the phrase which reminds us that our days are protected & blessed way beyond anything that we are able to do.

CONSIDER THIS ON THIS DAY

playing church

SOME OF OUR DAYS are filled with a desire to get ahead, succeed and find someone to love for a lifetime, but those things take work. And in this society, who has time to give-give-give, when the joy is being on the receiving end?

God commands us to be fruitful and multiply, right? It is not speaking into just having children. That's physical. And God deals with us on the spiritual aspects of us growing stronger FIRST.

Most of us take that to only mean, GET MARRIED and have children. But the start of being fruitful means that each person MUST DO THE WORK REQUIRED PRIOR TO RECEIVING prosperous bounties.

In II Chronicles 7, there was an 8-day worship service after the Temple of God had been built and after Solomon had taken an entire day praying and preparing God's people for worship. The story shows us that as soon as we leave church, the realization of the worship service isn't about God, but the items He places in our days for us to achieve and succeed.

But still God remains waiting for His children to be open and honest in worship at church & at home. II Chronicles 7:14 isn't a rally cry, but directions and information toward all of God's children becoming fruitful and multiplying & spreading the truth to others and bringing them into the church and increasing the family of God. The problem arises out of only wanting to be around God in the building, while ignoring His presence during all the other activities we actively participate; as if He turns a blind eye to our living a lie.

The choice is yours to make . . . be real or keep playing.

Read II Chronicles 7:1–16

Make this day the day you choose create more positives in your days which prepares you for your impending blessings.

CONSIDER THIS ON THIS DAY

I mind waiting

SOME DAYS ARE FILLED with abject hopelessness and the thoughts of giving up and walking away from direct challenges to our faith, what we think and life choices made.

If there is that one hope that we all should have in this life, is that the promises of God never leave us without absolute belief in walking out upright from the darkest tunnels.

Some hate waiting for change because it takes too long to mature. Others openly hate listening and take off walking with no direction.

Only a few mind waiting because they have realized that waiting is not the battle, but the preparation to do greater things and become better at listening and reacting.

In Romans 15:13, Paul leaves a prayer leaving no room for doubt in searching the abilities of God. He invokes the knowledge that when we pray for one another it should be done with fervor and love. No one waiting for rescue wants the five-minute sermon. No one wants to hear pity-filled stories in moments of grief and stress.

What they want is reason to wait on the Lord.

Give them that one thing and them let the Spirit of God do her job.

make this day the day you sit back and tell God . . . speak into my soul Lord.

CONSIDER THIS ON THIS DAY

validated

Over the past months and weeks, there has been people constantly decrying a standard of Christianity, which only calls for a select populous of the world's citizens. This is based on appearance and pedigree.

This Christian walk has a great deal to do with a changed and determined heart. The knowledge of Christ has been so deeply intertwined with politics, the rational minded have fallen prey to believe the words of men, over the Word of God. Translation after translation of Bibles have been written and some things have been omitted or rewritten to suit those who have financed the publication. BUT there is one thing that cannot be changed

GOD IS GOD ALL BY HIMSELF

In Mark 12, scribes and Pharisees decided to challenge Jesus' doctrine based on what they knew against how one should live. Jesus did not totally shut them down until He exampled a woman who had just given her all in dedication to a God who had blessed her with life and love.

Self-worth is validated by experience and not by the accumulation of stuff, nor one's place in society. Validation in Christ comes when one has totally given over and accepted Jesus as Lord and Master.

Those who chase a political Jesus have missed the mark and will continue to look at the ground. Those who have Read the Word and accepted it as truth, realize that Jesus came for all and not a select few. These are those people who liberally give love at every turn of the day . . . these are those HE will accept.

CONSIDER THIS ON THIS DAY

Read Mark 12:18–44

Make this day the day you decide to stand and accept the validation of Christ Jesus in your day and then watch how much more you are blessed.

CONSIDER THIS ON THIS DAY

that empty feeling

YOU ARE NOT ALONE!!!

God will provide you all that you require to be successful, strong and sure.

Believe that He is a rewarded of those who diligently SEEK Him.

Ask Him to move in your life in ways which will allow you to learn of Him better. That empty feeling is that place where you should regroup and gather all your emotions to take steps in gaining control.

He is with you!!

> Read Psalm 40 and then realize that
> you are not far from the top of the mountain

CONSIDER THIS ON THIS DAY

Running for nothing

THESE ARE THOSE DAYS in our lives that we must move with distinct purpose and determination.

God has granted us with certain talents and gifts so we can be successful in this life, while living the example of being that SALT around our friends and family.

The race we are on is ours specifically.

Not one single person can take any steps for us, breathe for us or sweat for us. This is our race alone. Whether the burden we are carrying is the load of issues covered with depression, anger, bouts of loneliness, gluttony, issues with sex and lies; it is ours alone to carry. It is ours alone to carry when we feel that we cannot make it to the next minute, next hour, next day or the next month . . . YOU have made it. And you have made it because you have been granted those certain talents and gifts to run your race at your pace. Not one person can take away the blessing that God has placed at the top of your hill and your mountain.

On this day, face your mountain and climb it or run up that single path that you know God has called you to follow. Run that path with the power that only you can feel that is being poured into you by God and God alone. A friend's advice is fine, but it is just advice. You take that advice and how you feel about yourself and bring it to God in the midst of running up your hill and listen for his direction on how to take your next step, your next breath, your next hurdle, your next detour.

You are not weak, you are not a sorry person, you are not the failure others may call you or cause you to think. YOU are a Conqueror in Christ Jesus

Run . . . Run because you have the power to achieve all that is in you.

Run . . . Run because you have made it passed half way and need to see things through.

Run . . . Run because you need to be the SALT and prove all haters wrong.

Run . . . Run because you have been blessed to endure your race to the end.

Run . . . Run because not one person can detour or deter you from you appointed goal.

Run . . . Run because quitting should not be one of your options.

Read 1 Corinthians 9:22–27

Make this day the day you decide to take that first step toward completing the goals you have laid down because of other folks and open yourself up for God to use you and all your talents to gain your blessings and your success.

CONSIDER THIS ON THIS DAY

time to make some moves

THESE ARE THOSE DAYS in our lives that we move with purpose & determination.

Stepping out of the cycle we find ourselves and reasoning on those things that are desired as goals and comparing our dreams to where we are to where we should be and want to be (take a breath here) It is time to make some definite changes in habits, behaviors and often repeated decisions; expecting better outcomes but still moving in the same steps.

It will never work.

God has granted us certain talents and gifts so we can be successful in this life, while living the example of being the SALT around friends & family. But in front of them, we hold back and never say or show the power God has given us because we fear being shot down by their limited knowledge of our growth in Christ

This race we are on is ours specifically.

Not one person can take steps for us, breathe for us or sweat for us. This race is ours alone. Once we realize that the paths we take cannot accommodate friends and family, we must take those steps which allow us to become a better person on our own. I am not telling you to cut them off completely, but there is a time in which you as an adult must do adult things alone with God.

On today, face your mountain, face your fears and climb out of the cycle that has been keeping you down through using the power God has put in you.

TIME TO MAKE SOME MOVES

You are not weak, stupid or sorry—because certain family & friends get upset because you are making moves to better your days, but a conqueror in Christ.

You will make it!!

Read 1 Cor. 9:22–27

No one person in this world can be you or hear those things God has given to you. It is your race to focus on and the blessings from truly focusing on your race are yours to enjoy.

***make this day the day you decide to open up and trust God to move you to better days.

CONSIDER THIS ON THIS DAY

on with the show

Burdens, bills, problems and advice from family and friend carry a great deal of extracting power.

All of them seem to work in unison to remove the little focus and drive we keep trying to muster to make it through the day, let alone the week. It seems that everyone else desires to have center stage in the things that we must deal with and overcome. And to top it off, they work to silence our voices by screaming at us because they feel that the little they know can somehow best work in our days, while they do not handle their own problems.

This little light of mine—that is based on a personal relationship with God, right?

In making and praying on future plans, it always seems as if something or someone is standing behind the curtain to throw a wrench or monkey into our show.

Our show, Our Show is just that: OUR SHOW.

Each of us have been blessed with great talents and gifts. When time avails itself for us to step up and move in our gifts, we are visited by people who seem to always fail at using their own gifts and talents, so they rain on our show adding unmerited burdens and negative speak / talk into our days. Why do we accept it?

In Matthew 11:29, Jesus gives us the best advice in moving forward in our shows and being blessed, "follow His example and mimic His attitude toward making the show easy flowing and great." After moving on

His word, Phil 4:13 pushes us to believe what Jesus stated in Matthew as solid gold.

So why carry the burdens as a flag?

Take control of your show. Ask God for clear direction and move forward and live with deep smiles.

Read Matthew 11:29

Make today the day that you open up and trust God to put you in the spotlight and then you perform to the best of your abilities.

CONSIDER THIS ON THIS DAY

taking responsibility

AS A PERSON WHO makes the statement claiming to be a Christian, it should be my main objective to live, walk and talk in such a way anyone who sees or hears me in a crowd, can recognize THAT CHRIST JESUS IS IN ME.

If, IF I become stress and act uncharacteristically out of turn, it's no one else's fault but my own. The devil did not make me do it. It wasn't caused by hormones, lack of money or car problems.

If a person calls themselves a follower of Christ all aspects of their days must align to that testimony.

One cannot be afraid to claim the trek they have chosen

I must be better and stronger than the people around me. I MUST BE THE SALT in my community.

I claim Christ Jesus on this day.

Read Romans 1:16

CONSIDER THIS ON THIS DAY

pure reflections

SOMETIMES IT IS HARD for any of us to accept the idea that we are full of faults and that the things we decide to do may not be 100% correct. Yet, we tend to make the wrong choices based on how our emotional state, how our circle of influence has pressed us to fall in line with the things they desire and oftentimes and by putting others ahead of ourselves at the wrong time.

The hardest parts of walking a productive and prosperous Christian life comes when we have to drop off some things we love to do and some friends, who for the most part, are only allowed around us for the good times. In other words, life has a way of forcing us to decide to choose the good over the bad.

Yet, we still try to hold onto the bad as if we can change some circumstances and people if we "will" it to happen.

In Job 13:15, Job makes the best statement any human being on this earth could make when it comes to the relationship between believer and God. In the middle of frustrations, the realization comes when we open our mouths to speak and those things we truly believe flow out like hot water from the tap. Job's response was open and honest and began and ended with him putting all of himself before God and His Standards.

Life is alReady hard enough, but to put all of our doings in the open and bounce them off of the levels of acceptance we know God wants, seems to make this Christian walk an uphill trek.

The reflections that we see within those hidden items that we hold so dear are those same piles of baggage which keep us from hearing so openly from God. Job understood that we all come short of being equal to God, yet it is the work of keeping our light so strong that we must take on this task of self-reflection to create a legacy for our children to attain.

The more days pass and the more we lean in on God's standards, the less difficult it becomes to look at our reflections and know that God will have the opportunity to tell the world, "have you considered my servant (insert your name here)"—(Job 1:8).

We do not have long on this earth and time for making a mess of those few remaining days seems so juvenile when eternity is the cost for missing the mark. Those things our children and friends say about us when we are not in the room should matter. If they don't matter to you, then how do you think God is taking that testimony, when those things done in our days don't line up with all the standards required by a Holy and Righteous God?

How does your reflection look after considering God is the final judge to your last destination?

CONSIDER THIS ON THIS DAY

it is fun being saved

Reference Scripture: Phil. 1:3–21

With all the things we have to deal with wrapped up in "what else could go wrong" on a minute to minute routine, we tend to take our position in Christ for granted. Yes, life is hard. But that is only on occasion and based in the choices we make that create some circumstances that spin out of control.

Yet when we stop, take a breath and then realize that all our steps are ordered by God. The repositioning of your feet for your journey and the taking of a good deep breath in the process of lowering of our blood pressure allows us to look toward the Heavens and thank God for another chance.

In the 1st chapter of Philippians, Paul and Timothy make every effort to detail the joys they receive, not only from knowing the people in the church at Philippi, but revel in the idea that they are going to see them again. But the strongest thing that is written is in the words, "in every prayer I make concerning you, I pray for joy." Not many people we know will look past their own struggles and ask God to bestow joy into the lives of those they care about; let alone those folks they do not see on a day to day basis.

Paul continues to detail the things that the church will face, when he compares it to those negative people he has encountered on his own Christian journey. In short, it is hard on some days to remain a dutiful Christian when you are bombarded by those who refuse to study the word, ask God for clarification of those things others have spoken into their lives with certain twists and turns added where it relates to the fellowship between the believer and God.

It is the fellowship which allows the members of the church to mature in the word. Herein lies the main issue with a great deal of "Christians"; some only want to accept things that they alReady know and think is the total sum of Christian Knowledge. It is difficult to speak joy into the life of a person who alReady thinks they know it all (Proverbs 4:1–12).

The fun part of being a saved comes in the continued knowledge of the Holy Spirit constantly feeding us, taking care of us and then leading and teaching us how to walk better in this world in our preparation for the next. In this letter, one should experience the epiphany that all of this will end and the life we now lead is totally to get all the people we can to see the happiness that comes when living a life for Christ is taking and walked without worry of the day when all of this passes on. In short, it is better to live in expectation of meeting Christ in a face to face; rather than worrying about the stuff that will be left behind (Phil. 1:21 & Gal. 2:20).

No one can do your life better than you.

But when it comes to living a joyous life in Christ; that walk cannot be alone. We are social animals and crave distinct social intercourse in our pursuits of a good day. When we are wrapped in Christ, the fellowship of a brother / sister solidifies the activity of the Spirit in our days

---

Read Matt. 18:20

CONSIDER THIS ON THIS DAY

it is fun being saved

Reference Scripture: Phil. 1:3–21

WHAT IS THE MAIN reason why you come to church?

- Is the knowledge that God will continually work for your good reason to become complacent in coming to church?
- How do you think gaining a better understanding of Christ and the history of the Early Church will aid you in your Christian walk today?

Since we know Paul was in prison in Rome, why do you think his central focus was on Christ? Can we say he was afraid to die, bored or just writing letters to pass time?

Does his wanting the best for friend and family ride higher than his situation?

Does it not seem crazy for a person to wake up in the mornings, knowing they will have a rough day, yet you see them with the biggest smiles?

I asked this to ask you, where does your joy lie, in a good check with 33 hours OT, your favorite team winning the big game 6 years in a row or your partner treating you MORE than special every day?

Happiness is defined as a state of being cheerful, happy, or in good spirits (feeling).

Joy is defined as a state of mind and an orientation of the heart (behavior).

CONSIDER THIS ON THIS DAY

there will be no stupid people in Heaven

Life can be a difficult and hard uphill climb. But that can be solved by the preparation and understanding the challenges faced when beginning each day and taking on certain tasks and gaining from opportunities that arise from contacts and hard work.

Let's look at it is in this manner:

1. To become a good husband / wife—a person must become willing to learn how to keep the other person happy and be honest in all things and in everyday so the entire house can function within the desires for prosperity and hope that if things start to fall, the other person has the faculties to pick up the slack

2. To become a good employee—a person must arrive at work on time and follow all the rules and regulations given by that employer to gain and maintain a constant paycheck

In the opposite manner, things fall apart in life when there are dumb decisions taken to try and gain certain things quickly and not truly work for them and stupid actions completed in an attempt to "get back" at someone and that entire action backfires and causes a boatload of trouble and destruction in the house, at the job and in good relationships

At no point in our lives can any one person change the boundaries and standards that God has set in place to bless all of creation to be safe and prosperous for selfish gains and those actions last.

Stupid actions begin with a person being filled with pride and arrogance—thinking and feeling that they know it all and the consequences can be dealt with at / on their own terms and that is never the case

This is why I can say that there will be no stupid people in Heaven.

There will be no stupid people in Heaven because those who will be in Heaven have Read and accepted His Word and understand that 'the fear of the Lord is the beginning of wisdom and that all things begin and end with Him.

Why would it make sense to try and better the things that God has put in place?

When is it possible for a person to change the standards that God has put in place greater and more life sustaining after making silly and dumb decisions?

I am not saying that one person is smarter than another, but when the choices are made to allow God to enlighten their daily walk, the percentage of stupid decisions falls close to zero, right?

Reference Scriptures you should Read:
Proverbs 1:7, Proverbs 4:1–12, Proverbs 2:1–6, Psalms 1

Make this day the day you choose to trust God for the directions in your life above the advice of friend and family, because man can and will fail—but the wisdom and grace of God is unlimited.

CONSIDER THIS ON THIS DAY

I am not who they say I am

SOMETIMES PEOPLE TELL US to shake off the haters and their words. Let's face it, sometimes their words cut more than their backstabbing actions. And those same words ALMOST makes us doubt who we are and not believe that we can become that very person God created us to be

To shake off the hell that others try to speak into our days, we must first stop accepting negatives and stupidity as if it is fact.

1. Our believing in God and ourselves MUST BE PARAMOUNT

never, never allow anyone to dictate how strong you stand in the middle of your life . . . they do not own ANY PART OF YOU.

2. Take a breath a realize that stench in the air is the lies & hate trying to cultivate in your heart. Once you allow a clown to break your heart, you allowed a simple distraction to move you from your goals.

In Psalm 37, the writer tells us three things that should keep our focus on God and the things we work toward and pray over. He tells us that worry is wasting time, being jealous of negative folks is power draining and trusting in God will shed light on all the gifts and talents WHICH WE HAVE BEEN GIFTED FROM BIRTH. we are God's creation, blessed and wrapped in His grace. There is not one person on this Earth who should have so much power & control over our days, that we lose sight of Jesus in our walk, prayer and smiles.

A clown is defined as a performer, a mine, a person who imitates physical humor and offers distractions into moments of fantasy and imagination.

Life is real. Problems are real. Believing in yourself and TRUSTING GOD FOR YOUR INCREASES IN LIFE ARE REAL. Those clowns who offer distractions are temporary and stuck crying and doing the same routines. They work hard to move you into the fantasy that they ways of thinking and living and working are right & correct.

But the Lord is our shepherd and the way He moves in your days are strictly for you.

> Read Psalm 37

Make this day THAT day you look in the mirror, wipe off the tracks from those wasted tears and allow Christ to heal your heart. Leave the haters, the clowns and the naysayers at the amusement park holding the tickets you no longer accept.

CONSIDER THIS ON THIS DAY

take pause

As a Christian, the path I am walking in this life should be so well defined that those who know me take pause and consider the reasons why I AM FOLLOWING JESUS then take similar paths without trying to make me deviate from the direction HE HAS CHOSEN IN MY LIFE. This journey I am on, He has designed to become beneficial for me and I am to use it as my testimony of His greatness.

I am on a path to become greater in this life and be the example which causes my friends to see the positive glory and grace God offers daily.

Read Romans 8:27–32

Success is just a step away. Get up and move toward your blessings.

CONSIDER THIS ON THIS DAY

pretend you get up

Some, only some of the situations we have dealt with have caused us to think the sky had fallen and we considered giving up. Then there are those circumstances in which bad decisions have added salt into the alReady heavy situation, so we end up stuck in a repetitive, negative cycle

Friends, family and some fren-enemies add or lend in advice, but that only perpetuated and grew the situation.

So we sit.

And we sit.

We sit back, get comfortable in the same thing and somehow try to function in mediocrity and dream that one day—one day—somebody will come along and bless us with cars, money, a fine and smart spouse and a huge house.

Let's face it, somebody has alReady come by and given you the tools to get up.

Pretend you have taken a deep breath and decided to walk away from constantly being mad, disgusted and broken. Where does the next step begin?

In Acts 2, there is listed the story of a man who sat for years and had the power to move, but accepted the situation as the only way to live. He had options. The Apostles gave him no material wealth or advice. They simply told him to GET UP AND WALK.

Sometimes our blessings are right in front of us and obtaining them only takes getting up, walking into church and thanking God for the power to WALK AWAY FROM THE NEGATIVE SITUATION.

CONSIDER THIS ON THIS DAY

Stop pretending you want to be and get better.

Make this day the day you actually make the decision to and walk away from living a mediocre life and choose a life based in Christ.

CONSIDER THIS ON THIS DAY
I'ma do me

Reference Scriptures: Matthew 16:24–27, Psalm 128

THE CONCEPT OF THIS life is to get and gain all you can before your die. From the phrases of "just do it", "you are all you need" and "I am gonna do me" is the failure to realize that something and someone is missing.

There is no doubt in our minds that we do not control the things which take place in this world or those circumstances which occur because of bad and delayed choices. Ours is a life which should be centered on the things of God for the Christian to live a prosperous life. But failures come when we constantly think that being blessed in having a great deal of possessions over the fellowship of Christ in our lives.

God is more than the temporal blessing

We have an expectation that if we work hard and do what is right by our family and friends, then we are living a good life. And most people are happy to live a life of work, work, work and little play. At some point in time you should get tired of the hustle and games which go along with following the rules and standards of this world. Expectations only become real and transition into tangible goods when one can maintain focus and become diligent and disciplined enough to stick to one plan and one goal until it is fully completed. Half stepping only leads to more frustration and failures.

In Psalm 128, David is specifically speaking to the fathers and mothers when he describes the growth of the family, the prosperity which awaits the children, and the need to understand why they need a fellowship with

God. The prosperity only takes place because the all members of the family are working together and are centered on knowing who God is.

In David's explanation—No one is doing things on their own.

In Matthew 16:24-27—Jesus gives the basis for the successful Christian life, but many will Read the Word, hear the Word and then refuse to live by it because some things must be left by the side of the road. The biggest distraction the Christian has in following Jesus is the need to put Him second and then look at the need to get and gain more as the catalyst for following God, attending church, paying tithes and playing the game of learning the Word, but living for the world. To truly become stronger in the world is to let go of the pursuits of the world as being central to the need for living and enjoying life. God can deliver much more than you can get by working 50 hours a week, right?

There is no doubt in our minds that working hard offers great rewards. The bi-product of working hard under the standards of this world means a shorter life and more bills at the end of those things.

Make today the day that you choose to make the adjustments in your life to place God first and then see how being blessed by Him is long lasting and debt free.

CONSIDER THIS ON THIS DAY

I'ma do me

QUESTIONS:
　　What does it mean to deny yourself and take up your cross?
　　Do you struggle with old sins and think about them the moment you begin to pray?
　　In Psalm 128, is there a promise that those who fear the Lord will be rich? What does this promise indicate for the Believer?
　　How have you seen God provide for your material needs in the past?
　　Are you prone to worry about the future? What are your concerns for moving forward?
　　How would placing your focus on God will change the way you feel about the unsatisfying areas of your life?

CONSIDER THIS ON THIS DAY

a gift that keeps on giving

Each day that we wake and then look in the mirror, there are those things that we see in us that are those subtle reminders of our parents. Those things they have said to us, those things they have done and didn't do for us. Some of them are heavy and have become a burden that we carry in silence, hoping one day to get over the scars which were left. In our attempts to be better and remove ourselves from negative feelings and patterns of the past, those things, that baggage is buried. Buried, but not forgotten.

In II Samuel 9, the story is told about the return of a gift David had received from his friend Jonathon. As king, David had the duty to rid himself of all the problems which should arise from friend, family and from the children of kings he had destroyed and killed in battle.

Oftentimes, we think of David as being a man above men, who loved God unconditionally. What we fail to realize is that David had to have a set of parents who instilled in him a sense of who he was in the eyes of a God who is continually faithful. Our lives can be looked on in this manner and questioned on what things we have gleaned from our parents and siblings, which cause us to take pause during certain actions of our day.

The gift of love and honor is something that has been buried in this society. We tend to seek to, "DO ME" above all that is right for our children and the future they want for themselves. So they pick up on all the bad habits we possess and then gift those things to our grandchildren. Yes, it is a cycle which can end by the time you've finished Reading this.

Most things which take place are set in us by the things we have seen, desired and gleaned. We often seek to repeat those things our parents have

A GIFT THAT KEEPS ON GIVING

done, because they seemed right and correct for a specific situation. But why should we seek to repeat the same steps our parents and older siblings have taken?

Separation Anxiety is defined as the fear (disorder) of being separated from something or someone who is a major attachment figure.

Sometimes, it is hard to separate from what we know to be comfortable. That is the hard part about being a Christian; we are called to be more than conquerors in all areas of life. The failure comes because we choose not to take steps toward winning daily battles and we settle for mediocrity.

In the middle of the 9th chapter, David has found Jonathon's son and looks passed the issues that may reside in him and offers him grace and a way to become separated from the things of his past. This is the same separation Christ offers to all who will fully accept the responsibility of becoming and being a Christian.

The choice is always up to you. Remain in the cycle that you have witnessed or take the path that is now before you.

Read: II Samuel 9:1–13

CONSIDER THIS ON THIS DAY

a gift that keeps on giving

Questions:

After having gone through the story of Mephibosheth, where can you place yourself in his circumstance?

What are the problems associated in trying to live life in the same manner as our parents and older siblings?

Would you approach a failed situation in the same manner as David did when it comes to old issues your parents had with other folks? Can you reach out to end old beefs and offer Christ?

With a mind of Christ and a willingness to change the paths and blessing in your life, the following bullets provide steps to see a clear walk. Do you believe that those bad habits our parents had are engrained in you?

- seek out our enemies and seek to bless them.
- look for the poor, weak, lame, and hidden to bless them.
- bless others when they don't deserve it, and bless them more than they deserve.
- bless others for the sake of someone else.
- show the kindness of God to others.

What are the major obstacles in you reaching your goals and becoming successful in Christ and in the world?

CONSIDER THIS ON THIS DAY

drop what you know

Reference Scripture: Luke 19:1–10

As a Christian, there should be this desire in you to do and be better every day. Gaining information is easy, when we sit back and allow others to fill our ears, minds and hearts with the things that they feel I relevant to our personal situations. We sit under pastors and politicians and teachers and friends and then fren-enemies, listening & accepting all the things they are spitting at us.

Some have beautiful voices, which sway crowds. Others have the gift of gab, filled with emotional stories. While others just bombard us with facts upon facts.

There has to be those days where the Christian takes a step back and realizes that this fellowship with Jesus is personal & should be approached in that manner.

In Luke 19, there is an account of a man who refused to just accept the words of others about Jesus. He decided to break away from the crowds to see things for himself and came away with a greater experience by stepping out in his desires and faith.

Most days are passing way too fast for us to just accept any word about the HOWs & WHYs affecting our lives. It is time to do the research on our own, because so much is dependent if we choose wrong or right with the information thrown at us at such a rapid pace.

Just like Zacchaeus, find that one high spot in your day and see if you can spot Jesus in the crowd of people who are offering advice about you & the Lord.

Find that high spot in your day so you can begin to recognize that it is time for you to transition upward in your life.

CONSIDER THIS ON THIS DAY

drop what you know

QUESTIONS:

What is your definition of the following words?

Patience—

Determination—

Satisfaction—

Understanding that growth is a process which causes the believer to shake off and drop off certain things in life, what are the situations which can cause a believer to pick up old habits and visibly walk away from Christ?

Write a mission statement for your life:

"*A mission statement is a summary of aims, goals and values of an individual*"

Example:

I am a committed recreational skater's advocate. I will do everything in my power to ensure that novices achieve the most positive first experience possible. This means encouraging them to buy the best equipment they can afford and to learn the basic skills, especially how to use the heel brake. To fight skate bans due to congested popular trails, I will help more experienced skaters build their speed and hill skills so they can train on a wider variety of trails without the risk of alienating other users. I will continue to encourage all skaters to improve their skills so they can adopt a well-rounded inline lifestyle.

CONSIDER THIS ON THIS DAY

un-friend me

THERE IS A TENSION that exists between friends. It is a line that is frequently crossed and contains understood limits in conversation, jabs, cursing and the occasional lie. But even these boundaries fail and friendships end.

Some standards should be held differently for those of us who call ourselves Christian, but it too fails in comparison to what the world will accept. So too the Christian misses the mark, because they want to be accepted by the world over the full acceptance of the standards of Jesus in their days.

In I John 4, we are told that we are liars because of consistent and repetitive actions of hate toward those who we refuse to call brothers and sisters. So, we un-friend them based on political standings and cultural background; walking away carrying the serious load of anger, hate and resentment. Friendship should mean something more than being in agreement.

Missing the mark is not hard when the things we put on the forefront of life benefits us the most. Being conservative in the areas of following Christ's examples of love, only waters down the testimony that we have said over and over again; OH, how I love Jesus.

In Matthew 5, the description is given of the American landscape and how the entire country has missed the mark and calling of Jesus. Some feel that they deserve the best of life based on financial standards. Others feel that they deserve a pass because of the areas they live in. All of this is earthly and will cause an entire family to lose out on the call to repentance because one person years ago was mad at someone else. Talk about a generational curse: "I am made at your family, because my grandfather didn't like them—reasons unknown, but anger still carried.

And we call ourselves Christians.

Read I John 4:20–21 & Matthew 5:22–24

Make this day the day you seek to do better by Jesus' standards and not the world. Call and heal old wounds and breakdown walls that the enemy (Satan) has enjoyed in separating the churches of God.

THURSDAY

NOTHING BECOMES HARD UNTIL YOU SAY AND BEGIN BELIEVING IT

CONSIDER THIS ON THIS DAY

something to fight for

THE IDEA OF HAVING to give up on obtaining certain things in life is an easy option for some people, but then there are those who refuse to give up without seeking out additional options.

The notion to consider failing never should be on the table when the best option is to take things to the Lord in prayer. But most of us don't. We'd like to handle everything by our own might and intelligence.

Some people desire to have the ownership of a house, a great looking car and the hand of someone who will love us beyond all the faults we try to hide from public view. These desires are tiring when we work extra hours at work, try to pinch and save for that down payment which is supposed to be the jump off point toward a good life. But it seems like the money in the savings account never increases. And all the hours at the gym is not attracting the person we dream to have in our lives.

In the first chapter of I Samuel, the writer introduces us to two women; the first, who seems to have it all. While the second; who seems to have gotten the short end of the stick and struggling to keep her sanity. The difference in the two can be summed up in one word—FOCUS.

Struggles in the daily grind can go on from week to week and then erode into month to month. Our response is not in the pain surrounding the situation, but the steps we should take in getting to the solution.

Hannah hurt enough that she did not lash out at Peninnah in response to the consistent ridicule and berating comments that she gifted Hannah, undoubtedly had taken place each day of the week.

The first few steps in becoming successful is the how's and who you decide to fight and the depths of your tenacity. Yes, it is the area of focus you lean the hardest to seek blessing and breakthrough.

In Hannah's case, as should be ours, she prepared herself before going to God in prayer. When she did find herself Ready to discuss her issues with God, she did not discuss her plans, wants and desires with another person. She was singularly focused on giving up and giving over to the Lord. Sometimes the idea of obtaining certain things in life requires a moment of giving up. Especially when you realize that you cannot handle most things and most people on your own.

It only takes a few minutes, even a few days to find your focus and the assurance required to LET GO AND LET GOD.

Read I Samuel 1:1–28

Make this day that day you decide to stop trying to carry the world on your back and allow God to not only hear your pleas and cries, but take the pangs from your heart so you can hear what it is that He has to say in the matter of directions.

CONSIDER THIS ON THIS DAY

situations do make you YOU

Over months & years of going through the UPs and DOWNs life can sometimes throw and roll, it can be said that if you place your focus on the end or getting out of the storm, the pressures are not so hard to bear. Let me say it this way, if you place a determined smile on your face and your HOPE IN CHRIST, you can focus on the things you should take care of without the distractions causing you to slip up, curse & worry.

In Philippians 4, the Apostle Paul is admonishing the church at Philippi to look beyond the circumstances of the world and the situations of the day and have a consistent testimony to ALL THE PEOPLE AROUND. He reminds them that the peace God grants in the lives of the Believer is great than all things seen or felt.

The testimonies which we all are currently writing ARE SEEN BY EVERYONE. So why think, act and live life as if we will fail and fall apart?

We serve and trust in the ONE GOD who will give us the strength, directions and grace to climb to heights & successes very few people are willing to SHOUT and SING about.

QUESTION: if we can believe and get information from simple rumors and RUN WITH THAT INFORMATION, why is it so difficult to DELIVER OUR TESTIMONIES with the same intensity when we come out of the storms of life?

Read Philippians 4:4–13

CONSIDER THIS ON THIS DAY

make this day the day you decide to let all who see you, see the and know the reasons behind the way you live, breath and choose to move toward your goals

CONSIDER THIS ON THIS DAY

this chapter

THE CHANGES AND TRANSITIONS of life are alReady hard enough without someone outside of your situation trying to give advice based on the little they know of you. It is not a selfish idea or thought when you don't want to discuss the patterns of changes you are experiencing. Some folk just need to understand that it takes a little time to personally adjust to your decisions to leave some bad behaviors and negative people behind.

When a writer begins a new chapter, there are countless moments of staring and gazing at an empty page. But in that writer's imagination, the page is filled with character movements, scene changes and that hope that those who Read the final product can see the new images developed after the words have been put on paper.

The Apostle Paul discusses the purpose for the change taking place in the believer in the 5th Chapter of 2 Corinthians. And then delivers the reasons why God is so detailed in writing the chapter and verses in our lives in the way He does. In verse 12, Paul points out that the way in which we live is ridiculed by those who don't get why you have changed so much and why they point to how we look and not the changes that have taken place within our minds and hearts.

Life alReady seems as if it is a constant uphill climb. Then to have folks walk in the middle of your change and try to Read you as if they know the entire book that God has been writing about your life.

Not one person has the authority to step into the middle of a chapter and dictate the final outcome of the book.

CONSIDER THIS ON THIS DAY

Not one person should have the audacity to rewrite portions of the chapter you are currently in and then refuse to either Read or listen to the beginning of the book called YOU.

Your response to all of their efforts is to follow the directions of the 5th chapter and become the living testimony of the changes mentioned about you in the 17th verse. Let them experience the new you. Let the see the Christ in you and allow them to understand that all the drama, all the sorrows and tears and then all the joyous laughter you are now carrying around as a result of the life editing work God has done in your story.

Read 2 Corinthians 5:1–18

Make this day the day you take the pen out of everyone else's hand where it concerns the directions God has written on your heart for His Purposes.

CONSIDER THIS ON THIS DAY

accepting all deterrents

Reference Scriptures: Proverbs 1:1–9 & 4:1–12

Here we are in a world where the bold Christian is scared to live and speak the word of God, because someone may be offended, either by the actions, the beliefs or the just hearing the word and having it invade their souls.

Here we are in a world where being politically correct is supposed to be the norm, but that changes the moment one person screams that they feel violated by a belief system they say is outdated.

In basic terms, these folks are fearful to live to a higher standard.

The term to fear the Lord simply means to live in dRead and awe of His total being. This causes the believer to have a desire to become more and more like the Lord is.

What the Christian should realize is that we serve a God who is omnipresent, omniscient and all powerful. He is not a fairy tale that can be wished away because some say that they refuse to believe in a God they cannot see or hear from. That is their choice. Our choice is to live in respect for all that He can do and that He will do in the lives of all creation; whether they believe in Him or not.

In Proverbs 1 & 4, Solomon makes the claim of how to approach and then live in fellowship with God, with an open mind and a child-like heart. It is in that approach the Christian should take the correct steps in learning of and hearing from God as if it is the beginning and we are learning things

all over for the first time. But that takes discipline and this world is so far removed from a disciplined life that it is almost laughable.

Here we are in a world that does not take God seriously, but wants the blessings of God to be there because they can eat, breathe and work. Every creature on the planet can do that. The difference between the believer and the non-believer is the believer tends to take on more of God's character and walks in less fear of the world.

For you to get passed the point you find yourself today, is to begin to realize that you have nothing to be fearful of and all things to gain. The world will tell you that your socio-economic status limits where you can and cannot go. The word of God tells you that you are more than a conqueror and that you can do all things any time of the day and any hour and in any minute that you decide to put feet to the faith that you claim you possess.

CONSIDER THIS ON THIS DAY

accepting all deterrents

QUESTIONS:
Is there a possibility that the people who attend church don't take God seriously?

What kinds of actions demonstrate that the individual takes God seriously?

Check the areas of your life in which you welcome and honor God's presence and rule in your life:

- ☐ family
- ☐ church
- ☐ career
- ☐ hobbies
- ☐ social life
- ☐ entertainment

Why is fear of the Lord the beginning of wisdom? Check any evidence that you are living in fear of the Lord.

- ☐ I take God's word seriously by Reading and obeying it
- ☐ I seek to align my life with God's will
- ☐ I seek to grow in Christ-like character and conduct
- ☐ I view God with a healthy sense of dread and awe that leads me to see worship

CONSIDER THIS ON THIS DAY

☐ is a different light every Sunday
☐ My testimony speaks out about my belief in God
☐ I come to church because I don't want to miss out on a blessing
☐ I follow God because I don't want to fail

CONSIDER THIS ON THIS DAY

taking what is yours

DOES IT NOT SEEM kind of strange when we run into people who are educated and talented, yet they are still living a mediocre life and do not have the drive to do anything within their talents and gifts?

We heard it time and time again, the only thing which holds an individual from achieving and obtaining is that on little thing that rests within them. No matter how much encouragement given, they seem to bask in the glory of not doing so they won't be called a failure.

Is that the one thing holding you back, someone calling you a failure?

In the first chapter of Joshua, we discover that Moses had died and the children of Israel were without a leader for the first time in 40 years. Not only did they not have a leader, their access to God was cut short. But God had made provision in the case something did happen to Moses. He had created the man of Joshua—attitude and all. He was chosen by God.

God had a conversation with Joshua in the first nine verses of this chapter and gave him all the tools he would require to take all that was promised to the children of Israel. After having repeated the promises that He had told to Moses, God filled Joshua's ears with them again and then added, "be of good courage." What is it that hinders and retards our flow forward in life, even after we have prayed and cried and then God answers?

Ours is a cynical life. We ask for things then we refuse to take the steps or try to achieve the littlest of successes because of fear someone will see us leaving their circle of influence or stuck in the pattern that if God blesses us, we must wait on family to make the decision to follow us as we follow God's call in our days.

Look at it this way, Psalm 115:16 tell us that all things on this Earth were created by God for human consumption, protection and control. But failure arises because the lack of courage and the ability to believe in self.

The time has come for us to make the decision to either believe in God and His promises or to walk away and accept being a quitter. Courage is that animal that will force you to run straight ahead and only question your steps once you have reached your goals. If you have prayed and thought over certain paths of action, what is causing you to drag you knuckles in pursuit of what God has granted in your life?

If God has promised it, where is the failure originating?

Read Joshua 1:1–9, Psalm 115:16, Matthew 6:26

CONSIDER THIS ON THIS DAY

taking what is yours

QUESTIONS:
In Matt 6:26, Jesus directs those who are listening to Him to look up in the skies and see exactly the birds in creation are doing.

"Look at the birds of the sky. They don't sow or reap or gather, yet your Heavenly Father feeds them. Are you not more than they?"

If God has an invested promise to keep to us, how do the birds demonstrate how to actively wait on the Lord?

What is the difference in active waiting and passive waiting?

What are you waiting on from God? Is it active or passive or just procrastinating?

Read Joshua 1:1–9.

What phrase did God repeat to Joshua over and over? Why did He emphasize this phrase?

After your morning prayers and getting Ready for work, what task has God been pressing you to be strong and of good courage to handle?

CONSIDER THIS ON THIS DAY

What are the challenges waiting for you if you decide to take the step toward taking what is offered to you from God?

Do you feel that living under God's rule is too large a task?

What do you require to motivate you in reaching the task and believing all things are in God's control?

CONSIDER THIS ON THIS DAY

obtain your authority

Reference Scriptures: Ephesians 1:3, Exodus 7:1–5

In living in the cynical world, we find ourselves being pushed and directed to accept the current status of life that we were born into. And some days we agree by giving up and walking away just to avoid a storm, not deal with certain friends and family and then force ourselves to think that we have just won a victory because we avoided a confrontation.

That is quite the wrong direction.

God has created each of us to be great and more than sufficient in the little gardens of life we have been blessed to take tend. God intends for us to manage all the things we choose to take into our days and claim them as our own. We become angry when things do not fit the ideals and dreams we thought we had placed in our plans for success. The problem lies is within the ideals we want and the reality that happens to fall in our laps: nothing is set in stone.

The largest problem is that we trust everything that stands before our eyes and we fall short to see those things God has laid out before us. We choose to listen to and hear all the things friends and family have to say concerning our future, the movement of the Holy Spirit in our lives and who we should trust with the love in our hearts.

We have a perception problem.

In Ephesians 1, Paul addresses the church at Ephesus with a greeting that should have created a pumped heart in each believer who Read and heard the words, "you are blessed in Christ with every spiritual blessing in the heavens."

We have a perception problem because we fail to realize that the moment we accepted Jesus as Lord and Savior, all of the spiritual blessings were unlocked in us. In Christ Jesus, we are granted the gifts of forgiveness, love, redemption, a position in His Kingdom, an eternal inheritance, healing, and authority to take command of every situation we face.

In Exodus 7, Moses was given authority to complete a task no other was qualified to do. He was gifted the ability to move with authority over Pharaoh and the power to walk into the palace of Pharaoh without wavering in his stance. God empowered Moses to do His will and complete His purpose in this world. Though Moses balked at the idea of leading God's people out of Egypt and returning to face the man he had called brother for so long.

> Faith isn't measured by the state of your mind, but how much foot you're willing to put in the actions required—T. Evans

> Faith is taking steps toward your goals even when you cannot see the next step—MLK

CONSIDER THIS ON THIS DAY

obtain your authority

QUESTIONS:

What type of Spiritual Blessings has God alReady blessed all believers with?

Read Exodus 7:1–2

In what sense do you think Moses was to be like God to Pharaoh?

> *Ex. 3:11: Who am I that I should go to Pharaoh and that I should bring the Israelites out of Egypt?*
>
> *Ex 4:1: What if they won't believe me and will not obey me but say, "the Lord did not appear to your?"*
>
> *Ex. 4:10: Please Lord, I have never been eloquent—either in the past or recently or since you have been speaking to your servant—because I am slow and hesitant in speech.*

We can see that Moses had an authority problem, what kinds of question or doubts do you have about leading in the domain where God had placed you?

Because God had alReady equipped Moses with all the tools needed to accomplish the task, what was left for Moses to do?

What is left for you to do?

CONSIDER THIS ON THIS DAY

stretching and exercising

AFTER DAYS AND WEEKS of doing the same exercises, the body becomes lacks and begins to return to the shape and sometimes the size that it was before the workout regime began. There is an order of creating and maintaining a steady progression toward successful growth and profits that is found in stretching the limits of the muscles which are contained in the body. This goes for the areas in life that we have yet to travel, understand or adventure into.

As time passes, we can sit back and meditate on opportunities that have been missed, kicked to the side because of laziness, procrastination or just the pure choice of not wanting to do better because living in mediocrity seems to be regiment of exercise that is suitable.

Once we have received Jesus as our Lord and Savior, there is that moment in which we feel all the power of the Holy Spirit and we can, not only feel the power, we gain an insight to the visions of our having successes in Christ Jesus. But two weeks after having been saved and attending church, listening to folks complain about the mediocrity of the church and the pastor, we take steps to join in with the choir of "somebody should do something else."

In Matthew 20 and Proverbs 4, the writers show that there is a direct path out of living a negative and mediocre life that is steeped in doing what it takes to being a true Kingdom Individual. Sometime our lives must be completely shaken up, changed, broken and then rearranged to relocate us the place God wants us to be so we can not only see Him in our lives, but discover the purposes He has given all of us unique talents.

Matthew 20:25—the mother approached Jesus because she did not want her sons to live a modest life when the best catalyst was right in front of them. She wanted her sons to be seen as Jesus was being seen as a great individual. And Jesus' visage was based in His service toward the masses.

Proverbs 4—Solomon offered some harsh directives toward his sons and those who came after them as off-spring . . . he wanted them to stretch the limits of their minds by not only obtaining a good education, but garner the distinct ability to use all that they learn so they could serve one another and still be in line with God.

> "If you want and desire a happy life; tie it to a goal and not an object"—Einstein

We miss the mark of being a Kingdom Man / Woman because we put all our focus on stuff and not the source or the standards required to mimic the source.

The greatest power and strong individual possess is the power to serve someone lesser than they are. So, what is holding you up from serving and then reaching your goals?

> Read: Matthew 20:25–28, Proverbs 4:1–8, John 13:1–5, 12–17

CONSIDER THIS ON THIS DAY

stretching and exercising

QUESTIONS:

In what ways have you seen men dominate people in the church?

Have you ever felt or been tempted to dominate others? If so, in what sphere of influence?

What stopped you from doing it?

What things do you do which cause you to take pause in moments like that?

How does Jesus' actions in John 13 relate to the reference scriptures?

In what ways are you currently serving others in the following areas?

What is one practical way you can serve in the following areas that you aren't currently doing?
Δ marriage / relationship Δ job
Δ parenting Δ church
Jesus has not stopped at washing feet . . .

STRETCHING AND EXERCISING

Philippians 2:6–8

Though He was God, He did not consider equality with God as something to be used for His own advantage. Instead He emptied Himself by assuming the form of a slave, taking on the likeness of men. And when He had come as a man in His external form, He humbled Himself by becoming disobedient to the point of His own death—even the death on a cross.

CONSIDER THIS ON THIS DAY

greatness defined in you

Reference Scripture: Matthew 20:20–28, Genesis 12:2, 2 Samuel 7:9

IT IS NO SECRET that all of us crave to be on top of things, become successful beyond those in our circles of influence and accomplish that one thing which would set us apart from the crowd. And all of this could take place.

The items which stops us from having great relationships, getting the top ratings at work to garner that 8% raise and having good credit is based on the actions of sacrificing those behaviors, old friends and often brothers and sisters to reach the higher levels of talents and gifts we refused to use.

In Matthew 20:20–28, the writer details a brief encounter with a mother, who saw greatness in her children and wanted them to be at the highest levels she could possibly bring them. She brought them to Jesus and made her requests known. But in turn, Jesus didn't respond to her, but her sons—why?

We all have been pushed, cussed and fussed at when we have fallen short of certain goals and made bad choices which continually delay those successes we desire. Our parents can only take you so far in life. After that the questions rest at the feet of the individual, who should either step up, openly make the choice to take on the challenges of drinking from that cup of struggle to success or cower and return to mediocrity.

God has gifted each of us with great talent and the power to use it in a manner that will not only put us ahead of the crowd, but will allows us to teach & train others to get and gain as we are.

Make this day the day you step to Jesus and affirm your inheritance and blessings toward greatness.

CONSIDER THIS ON THIS DAY

greatness defined in you

Matthew 20:22–28

What did the mother of James and John as Jesus in the text?

What is the purpose of any parent in the regards to the lives of their children?

IF the request from the mother is to find greatness, what is right or wrong in this request?

How does the world define greatness?

God had made certain promises to Abraham and then repeated it to David:
I will make you into a great nation
I will bless you
I will make your name great
and you will be a blessing Genesis 12:2
I have been with you wherever you have gone
and I have destroyed all your enemies before you.
I will make a name for you like that of the greatest in the land 2 Samuel 7:9

Underline the common elements that you see in both the promises. What do you think of greatness now?

Where does it begin?

CONSIDER THIS ON THIS DAY
obtaining the rightful inheritance

Reference Scriptures: Psalm 24:1–4, Romans 8:19–22, Gen. 3:16–19

AFTER GOD HAD CREATED and placed His creation in the garden, He delegated the responsibility of caring and managing what belongs to God. What is strange and perplexing is the way in which the creation has taken ownership over things which could not be made by the hands of man.

This is the common problem of confusing stewardship with ownership. It is similar to a young adult thinking that their parent's house somehow belongs to them when they have not offered one hour of work, gave into and walked out of 15 stressful days of work and not paid one bill in the flow of maintaining the house or car.

In Psalm 24, David is openly showing the children of God that all things begin and end and belong to God without question and is Ready and willing to live a sold-out life for the Lord. By the time we get to verse four, the explanation and the standards are set on how one can approach God and receive the inheritance that He had created for all of creation to enjoy.

It should be our understanding that those things God has placed in creation for us; is for us and to be used, eaten and cared for. The only definite obstacle in any one person obtaining portions of their inheritance lies within their behaviors, beliefs and attitude in accepting the terms of the standards God has set for one to have a relationship with Him. It is straightforward. There are no gimmicks or hidden doors. It is for us to either accept the relationship fully or walk away.

Relationships grow in this way—there are some days when everything is roses and sunshine and then there are those moments when storms arise and one word spoken in the wrong tone sets off hours of arguing banter. Each of these is a cycle toward the partners growing into one another. Each must give up and give off something that will encourage the other to be and become better. But what is not understood in the growing of the relationship is that each person takes a large portion of the other person into themselves and assimilates the best while defining the foundation of the relationship.

In Romans 8:19–22—Christ gave and continues to give into the children of God. The problem again is that the children of God do not want to fully open up and obtain their rightful and righteous inheritance.

We make certain decisions during the daily grind that have direct outcomes that are not in the plans or will of God. And still He respects those and makes moves to bring us back to the right paths. And yet—we still either overshoot the landings or we just go off course and try God's patience . . . again and again and again.

The Questions:

"In Psalm 24—The Earth is the Lord's and the fullness thereof; the world and they that dwell there in."

> How does God's rule of the Earth and everything it contains relate to His directive for man to rule?

> How do you think most people feel about the privilege of ruling? Is it an arrogant take toward things?

> How do you know?

> How often do you think about the dominion God has given you to manage and lead?

☐ never ☐ sometimes ☐ daily ☐ only in the morning

> Can you describe a time when you were in charge of an area or event and you felt the weight of the responsibility of ruling (as a parent, supervisor, teacher or coach)?

OBTAINING THE RIGHTFUL INHERITANCE

Did this timing cause you to think on God being over you?

Think about the sphere of influence God has over you. In what ways do you feel your being faithful to carry out your responsibilities? In what ways are you failing to lead effectively?

CONSIDER THIS ON THIS DAY

greater than you think you are

Reference Scripture: Psalm 8, I Samuel 17:34–40

To UNDERSTAND THE GIFTS and talents that are inside of you, you must first realize that there is a defined purpose for your life.

It is not too rich beyond belief, be the best athlete on the planet or adorable and loved by everyone in the world.

Your purpose is to take care of and increase those things, people and children you have watching you on a daily basis.

Yes, God did give us all dominion and rule over everything in the universe, but as small as the human animal is compared to the universe; most of us better stick to the little world we call home & family.

In Psalm 8, David gives all thanks to God for taking His time to create man in His image, make Him just a shade lower than He is, and grant more into this little being than all others in the universe.

DO YOU GET MY POINT??

God created you to do great things and be a greater person. You are not as sorry and pitiful as some may have said. They didn't create you nor did they give you the gifts you are ashamed to use.

This should be that one day you choose to stand up and start believing in yourself and your talents because ALL OF YOUR GIFTS ARE DESIGNED TO SHOW THE POWER GOD HAS GRANTED IN YOU.

You are a child of the King of Kings . . . so start acting like it.

CONSIDER THIS ON THIS DAY

current and relevant

> Reference Scripture: Exodus 34:24–31

HOW IS IT THAT we seek to gain good and great things by never really wanting to do what is required to the next higher and greater phases / levels in life?

If we would consider our influences and abilities when we take the time to comfort and encourage those around us, exactly how much more would get done if our testimonies became as true as the Christians we imagine ourselves to be when we look in the mirror or at those times when we are the holiest person in a room of upset people? It is unmeasurable.

For one's testimony to become stronger, one must trust the system that God has put in place. And that in itself is a slow transformation because many of us like to skirt the rules and stretch the boundaries just for the sake of doing it. Then we miss out and don't know why.

In Exodus 32:23–24, we find that God had laid out specific guidance and obligations in the lives of the children of Israel. All of it was set in place so they would remain in the most fruitful and prosperous places in the land that God has set aside for them. But like most of us, we don't want to be told what to do, when to do it or must give up any portions of ourselves to be and become better. We would rather low ball things and live a comfortable life. That means no stresses from having to learn new things, meet new people and God forbid . . . attend church on the regular.

We can say that it may be the fear of the unknown, but in dealing with God, it falls in the realm of not being able to trust God to keep His promises.

In the directives in Exodus, God required the men to meet with Him three times a year. On the backside of this, He promised to increase their land and belongings so greatly that they would not have to worry about home when they were in worship with Him. He basically told them, "I have your backs."

How is it that we seek to pray, get and gain and never take a moment to trust God to take of the little things that He has alReady promised to do?

The simple answer falls in the lines of either not wanting to do a thing, not caring about what is taking place and thinking that time is "on our side", and the belief that we are invincible and can make this journey based on the little things we know and the simplistic talents we have.

CONSIDER THIS ON THIS DAY

a point of no return

> Read Ezekiel 22:1–31

Another year has crossed the half-done mark, and some of us are in the same pit we were in at the start of the year and carried over from three years prior. Still filling the pit in with diminished hopes and dashed dreams.

What is the cause of this yearly cycle?

In Ezekiel 22, God is talking to the prophet about the problem of discipline, focus, respect and reverence. The same issues we have in many families these days. Ezekiel is given a tour of the history of the families he has been giving the Word of God and those God has been watching. He (God) then asks several times, where are the men who should love Me and direct their children toward Me?

Disappointment comes when we realize that God is not pleased in the actions or inaction His children take in not raising strong and determined children.

He is looking for KINGDOM MEN AND WOMEN.

This world is eating up our children and for some reason, the church has decided to deliver & accept mediocrity. We allow negative and lazy people to dictate away the directions of God for limited successes and borrowed hopes.

The quality of lives of our children should be paramount. Our lives in front of God should be better than the people who came before us.

The problem is NO ONE WANTS TO BE HELD ACCOUNTABLE. We choose weak people to follow in church, knowing that they are not sold out for God and this allows us to have an out and quickly quote, "you cannot judge me." . . . . allowing Satan to walk in and dictate how much further your family will fall away from God.

So, our children suffer. And they suffer greatly, because they don't know God like they should because our testimonies just don't line up on any level. Meaning we don't live up to being the great parents and Christians we see in our heads. We fail because we don't want to listen and then we do not want take any instruction which is going to cause us to have to do any type of work or leave certain pleasures behind.

With decisions like this—our kids suffer

Our children suffer because they are not prepared for the future or how to deal respectively with God or with the people they must go to school with or work with later on in their lives.

We must do better.

At some point in time we have to see that there is a point that God will allow the world to beat us up to turn us around, but some of us are so hardheaded, we cannot hear God or see the constant signs of Him wanting us to do and be better.

CONSIDER THIS ON THIS DAY

shut down but still able & willing

> Reference Scripture: Acts 4:1–31

LIFE THROWS A BUCKET of mess at us on a daily basis. Sometimes it feels like 10 are thrown at the same time and from odd directions, like friends and family, who smile and go on as if they are supposed to challenge our salvation and hope in God.

BUT GOD gives us so much more to hang onto and hope in that shutting us down for a moment ONLY INCREASES THE REASON FOR A DEFIANT TESTIMONY.

In the 4th Chapter of Acts, we find that Peter, John and the 40-year old man, who was lame, have been locked up for a night and threatened with their lives if they spoke of THIS JESUS AND THE SALVATION HE OFFERS. The strongest examples come when each man opens up to the Spirit of God and refuses to stay silent in the midst of others not wanting, for the second time in two days, to hear or accept the Gospel of Christ Jesus.

What does it say about you to others if they not only see Christ in your daily walk, but hear your testimony in all the victories you face each week?

So I say to you on this day—choose the best weapon you have in your life and allow the Holy Spirit to add into your every step through every waking day so you can shake some hardness out of the lives of those hating on you and trying to shut you and your family down.

NOTES:

There are two things that we should look at in the matter of spiritual conversion:

1. How we move to God
2. How we move toward the world

What does hospitality mean in the Christian life and home?

The HOLDING CELL

Stocks—chained to the wall // chained to the floor

Limitations in dealing with church folk will limit where and how we can move in God

What is the emotional challenge to leaving the holding cell?

CONSIDER THIS ON THIS DAY

on the outside of God looking in

Reference Scripture: Acts 3:1–26

WE HAVE THOSE DAYS when things have been going very well and we can see the Hand of God moving across the situation we thought had the ability to be unending and drowning.

In our stepping aside and allowing God to change us in little ways, we can see that the actions of those around us, mostly in church, becomes the distraction from you getting the next level or short term goal you have set for yourself. Above that the blessing God is now in question based on the jealousy of others, their unbelief and they're not having allowed God to be real in their days.

In the 3rd chapter of Acts we can see the events unfold quickly after the lame man has been granted a way out of his unending situation and the ability to immediately respond to God's blessing in the best way available; telling folks about God with a smile.

Joy comes the moment one realizes that the deliverance God is complete and requires nothing from us outside of letting go and believing. The hardest things for the Christian to is TRUST GOD and sit back and let Him work in their lives. If we look at this broken man at the Gate of Beautiful prior to his physical healing, we can take notice of those countless people who walked by and did nothing a sustaining effort to create positive feelings and ideas into this man. Yet they had strong words and question immediately after he had overcome the things which kept him sitting on the ground and watching life pass him by.

It is within us to do two things in other people's lives; encourage or destroy.

In taking the latter actions, God still does not remove Himself from the lives of those who do things to limit and destroy the progress of the Spirit in other folks' lives.

Yeah we know them. They praise God on Sundays, cuss, fight and fuss Monday through Friday, try to pray and get things right by nights' end on Saturday. But somehow they seem to keep God in a little container during those days and only opening this container when the bottom has fallen out on broken relationships, money becomes short or they cannot find relief from the stress which keeps them up all night.

Yeah we know them. They are the ones who have not one ounce of respect for their parents or any other person older than them, but they are quick to say that they are blessed and highly favored. They repeat the phrase, while in the middle of stabbing a brother or sister in the back because they refuse to pay monies they owe.

We serve a great God. He forgives us of all the things we have done. But we fail, like those in the temple to understand that the things Jesus went through was to fulfill the promises God made with Abraham—for all to be heirs to the Kingdom.

Yet, we need to understand that there are some who know God but somehow finds ways to keep from trusting Him for their deliverance. They are on the outside of life, watching God make great changes in the life of those who call on Him, have given up some negative behaviors and people to have the ability to enter church and praise God for being who He is in their lives.

CONSIDER THIS ON THIS DAY
the power is in us

> Reference Scripture: Acts 3:1–26

THE EXPECTATION OF LEAVING a consistent problem opens us up to the possibilities that we can learn something new from all calamities which befall us. The challenge is for us to have the desire, not only to leave, but have defined plans of not repeating the same circumstances which landed us in the problem we keep waking up and facing.

The expectations of leaving certain problems and situations weigh on us so heavily, that we sometimes choose the first option available. In other words, we know that there are some failures in certain options, which may be backed with strife, headaches and storms, but somehow we fall prey in thinking a different situation is better than the area we currently are struggling to survive through, in and around.

The power is sometimes in the amount of patience that we grow into.

In Acts 3, we find a man who had been stricken with an affliction from birth sitting at the place where all of God's children could enter the temple for worship and offering. This man was accustomed to his situation and was dropped off by those who knew him and were familiar with his problem.

They were limited.

In consideration of us being successful in this life, our paths are hindered by the things we believe, know and trust in. This is the age of information. A great deal of things are at our fingertips allowing us to research, gather and gain a little understanding. But it is a problem when we must lean on the God who gives us answers of His power as soon as each daily sun rises and sheds light through our window blinds.

It was not that Peter and John were there to just lift this man out of situation, but they were there to offer the answer to all the distractions which held the man's attention.

If we take a step back and look at all the things that we have allowed to pass us by because of some simple circumstances which had us tied up in emotional bondage, just think how much further in life we could be if we would have just fixed our eyes on God and the word He has been trying to put in our days for the longest time.

The answer is not what we can get from God, but how we get up, stand and then walk. The man was instructed to get up and walk. He was not told that there would not be any problems occurring in his life after his healing, but to rise and walk in the name of Christ Jesus.

There were no limits given in the instructions.

So, what is our problem from day to day in walking in the power of Christ Jesus?

CONSIDER THIS ON THIS DAY
looking for the immediate thing

> Reference Scripture: Acts 1:1–10

WITH THE CHANGES TAKING place in American society, what is the church to do in the face of knowing Jesus and the reasons behind his resurrection?

After all things had been completed, Jesus remained with His chosen apostles in preparation for their mission to deliver the Gospel message to a world that was dead set against anything heavenly. Here is the proof the gospel message go back to the apostles can be trusted: the apostles received it directly from Jesus. Evidence of the empty tomb and the resurrection appearances point steadily in only one direction: Jesus is alive!

But if we look at the scriptures, we can see that his own disciples still expected the temporal blessings over the eternal promises that Jesus kept speaking about. This is much like the people of God in today's society, we want to be holy, but God better give up some cash and a house and a nice car if we are to truly follow Him. In Acts 1:6–8, the questions arise and are answered with the commandment, "wait."

Does material possession equate the movement of God in the life of a Believer?

If we are to listen to those who call themselves Apostles and Prophets, much of their message all falls on the temporal blessings. Salvation is so much more than the supplying of physical need and greed (Matt 6:33). It is the gift of God that all should come to the knowledge of Christ Jesus and be saved, but this knowledge is habit breaking and life changing for those who truly want to live a better life.

Luke's review of life with Jesus after His resurrection and Jesus' command to wait for the Holy Spirit's coming (1:4–5; see also Luke 24:49). Jesus gave this same instruction on several occasions (not only one, as in the NIV). But if we are to wait on the Holy Spirit to indwell us; that change we are looking for only comes to fruition the exact moment we believe and begin to release all our unbelief, denial that He can do all things and trust in Him above all things told to us contrary to His Word.

It is a work in progress. We are a work in progress.

Patience is a hard habit to learn and practice. But once we can gain this habit, our outlook on life can become so much clear and bad habits are then seen as the distraction from us being prepared for better understanding how God speak to us and moves in our lives.

CONSIDER THIS ON THIS DAY

standing above all things

Reference Scriptures: Philippians 4:15–25

HERE WE ARE AT the end of the Letter to the Philippians and we should wonder what the main topic was as it were given to the church at Philippi—stand faithful and trust that the power of God will be strong enough to deliver you.

If we could rediscover something great in our days which would take us from the cycles that we are living today, what would that one thing be?

Now that you are looking back, can you see how many times God reached out and tried to pull you from destructive behaviors and bad choices?

If we should have a take away from this letter it should be that the faithfulness we show in all our duties, efforts, relationships and set goals is preeminent in us reaching success. Faithfulness takes effort and it takes each individual to a level of continued determination of stretching the limits of belief and hope. In becoming complacent one loses out of the talents and gifts that were granted at the beginning of life. To become better / stronger an open effort has to be that singular focus.

Question: Why is it so easy to put God's work aside to satisfy the things of the flesh?

Answer: Because it is easier to satisfy the flesh than satisfy the spirit.

Satisfying the spirit requires a determined mind; a set pattern of work and a desire to live by the standards of God and willingness to let those things people speak into our days not influence our self-esteem and self-efficacy.

Epaphroditus had a commitment which mirrored the commitment Jesus had when He went to the cross. He viewed his mission as more than just a delivery, as he was fulfilling the Lord's work. By completing this task which was entrusted to him the church at Philippi would glorify God.

Considering that, nothing was going to stop him! Imagine what type of advice we might (perhaps rightly) give a person today who experienced a severe sickness like Epaphroditus did. We would likely tell him to "slow down" and "take care." "Rest and get your strength back" or "You won't do yourself any good by stubbornly continuing this mission."

After all, "Paul will be fine" (Phil 4:11) and "He will understand your situation." We may say "The work of God is bigger than any of us just come back, get the proper help and let someone else do it" or "you need to be back with your family."

I can't find good grounds to argue with the spirit of this advice, yet the dedication Epaphroditus had to his mission would not have any of it. He chose God first and waited for his blessings.

CONSIDER THIS ON THIS DAY

who affirms you?

OVER MONTHS & YEARS of going through the UPs and DOWNs life can sometimes throw and roll, it can be said that if you place your focus on the end or getting out of the storm, the pressures are not so hard to bear. Let me say it this way, if you place a determined smile on your face and your HOPE IN CHRIST, you can focus on the things you should take care of without the distractions causing you to slip up, curse & worry.

In Philippians 3, the Apostle Paul is admonishing the church at Philippi to look beyond the circumstances of the world and the situations of the day and have a consistent testimony to ALL THE PEOPLE AROUND. He reminds them that the peace God grants in the lives of the Believer is greater than all things seen or felt. All movement forward in life is based on our mindset and how much we believe in our talents and gifts. The testimonies, which we all are currently writing, IS SEEN BY EVERYONE.

So why think, act and live life as if we will fail and fall apart?

The thing which should change our beliefs in ourselves is who we rely on to affirm who we are and how strongly we allow our hearts to lean toward Christ.

We serve and trust in the ONE GOD who will give us the strength, directions and grace to climb to heights & successes very few people are willing to SHOUT and SING about.

QUESTION: if we can believe and get information from simple rumors and RUN WITH THAT INFORMATION, why is it so difficult to

CONSIDER THIS ON THIS DAY

DELIVER OUR TESTIMONIES with the same intensity when we come out of the storms of life?

Read: Philippians 3:15–21

CONSIDER THIS ON THIS DAY

getting off our high horse

> Reference Scripture: Philippians 2:1–15

It does seem the older we get and the more we learn, we tend to take a great many things for granted. We move in and out of our busy days as if we control all the blessings which come our way.

We make moves like the totality of our gifts are the exact things which allows us to become greater in life and then good examples to those around us. The problem is that we forget that all things begin and end with Jesus' grace.

We walk passed people without any type of "hello or good morning" as if Christian Love is only for the people we know & fellowship & worship alongside of as "members of the body of Christ."

Success of any good organization, church or family is based on the actions which lead people to see our testimony up close and personal

In Philippians 2, the writer gives distinct reminders to the church, which no individual in church should feel that they are above reproach because of title, financial status or by the manner in which they feel they are "blessed and highly favored." The writer states that WE all should have the same mindset and that our thought patterns should resemble that of Jesus'.

Paul wrote this letter to let the church at Philippi knowing that the good work they were doing could be destroyed by having sorry and selfish attitudes.

QUESTIONS:

CONSIDER THIS ON THIS DAY

How does a person move forward in life and get out of their own way?

Why is it so difficult for people to take good, solid advice during their spiritual maturation?

CONSIDER THIS ON THIS DAY

just give up

Reference Scripture: Philippians 1:1–30

IN LIFE THERE ARE those items that either can cause us to be inspired to do and seek greater things or just look at tall the negatives and drag on and quit.

To achieve anything, it requires a belief in oneself and trust in all the things God can and will do through us in the middle of Him actively engaging in our lives. The first chapter of Philippians offers up an insight to the mindset of this church and how they wanted to be seen by all those around them in Italy.

In all accounts, the church at Philippi was the church plant of Paul's ministry and they accepted him and the Gospel with open arms and sought to increase their church fellowship, not out of love, but the knowledge and discernment of Jesus and the example He left for all of us to follow.

We, just like the members of the Philippi church, have been endowed with certain gifts and talents (fruits) which are fed by the movement of the Holy Spirit and how much we are willing to accept from Him as nourishment toward our becoming greater Christian magnets (Read John 15:46).

The time for growth within each of us is limited on the amount of time we are willing to feed into our fellowship with God and then how much of ourselves we are willing to allow God to use of us. Just as the exampled story in Sunday's sermon—the young boy could have just moved to the back of the crowd and kept those things to himself and let a great many people suffer because he either did feel good about himself or he was thinking, "those things that are for him are only for him."

Is this Christian Life one that we can quit and walk away from and be totally unreachable by God?

What is the outcome of having a growing fellowship with God and the Holy Spirit?

CONSIDER THIS ON THIS DAY
breathing deeply and correctly

Colossians 2:20–23 and 3:1–15

IN OUR MOVEMENTS THROUGH Colossians, we have discovered that it is our attitude and our belief patterns which can either move us closer to Christ or allow us to be convinced to see other directions available in getting eternal salvation.

In my Young Adult Bible Study, the question last week about being an heir to Abrahams covenant with God and a direct heir to receive God's grace and have the ability to walk into the Kingdom because we all are of the bloodlines from those who were slaves in Africa. This false assumption is based on the limited theology (belief) of the Jews and those who believe Israel have an open door into God and into Heaven. Believing this puts the individual under the 163 provisions written under the Old Testament Law. None of us could possibly live a strict life under these conditions to meet God based on obedience and faith without the blood of Jesus to redeem us from sin.

In this lesson we will move to understand why Paul wrote to the Colossians based on their emotions, faith and ability to fall prey to new forms of gospels which require additional patterns and steps in reaching Jesus and gaining salvation.

The Christian Life is a process. Our moving to better lives and becoming the Christians and adults we believe we are being a process and it takes some work. It is our direct attitudes which cause us to procrastinate and put off doing what is needed and required of us to reach those things we desire.

I have attached to articles for this lesson which deal with those "Dark Days" that all of us travel through from time to time. Please Read them so our discussion on Tuesday night will allow us to move a little deeper in Christ.

CONSIDER THIS ON THIS DAY

results matter

> Reference Scripture: Colossians 2:1–9

OUR APPROACH TOWARD FRIENDS and family do have a great weight on how successful they are in their attempts to either grow or reach the goals they have set for themselves & their families.

Not all our family members and friends seek to move above the stationed in which they have been living. It is our desires to see them reach for the skies, so we pray and hope and hope and pray that they do not remain stuck on slow & satisfied.

In the 2nd Chapter of Colossians, Paul is telling two churches that his prayers are set before the Lord concerning their successes in this world & that they become stronger in the Word. His example to us shows that visibility does not hinder a good prayer life and a short phone call or text to say—I am praying for you and your family.

Where we are in Christ has a great deal to do in how those who watch us move toward the church and then to Christ Jesus.

Our results in keeping those we know and love encouraged should be seen in the responses and blessings God pours out on us for being ACTIVELY FAITHFUL toward His children. For us to keep reaching and moving, we must take serious moments in our quiet time so we can remain rooted and grounded in all areas of our lives. Our ability to allow others to see Christ in us depends upon how much of us is NOT in God's way.

CONSIDER THIS ON THIS DAY

All the things that we would like to plan and do in the next 6 months and 6 years must be thought on, prayed over and planned-out to the simplest terms. If we do not begin now to set things in order, how will they work out when that they arrive?

CONSIDER THIS ON THIS DAY

worthless fruit

Scripture Reference: Matthew 21:18–22, Mark 11:12–14, 20–26

It is a matter of importance in our approach of the day. Those items we take from the prior day's challenges and the storms that we just walked through.

How we are perceived and what we can give to others would be the catalyst for them seeking more and more out of us. And to make them happy --> we gift them our last.

We achieve a few things and then we feel brand new and think the stench we are smelling is beautiful . . . but the entire time we are walking around with our heads up the wrong place.

Then we should ask ourselves, WHAT DO WE HAVE LEFT FOR GOD?

In both Gospels, Mark 11 & Matthew 21, the writer details the incident of Jesus seeking fruit from a fig tree and finding it void of fruit and filled with leaves. Jesus' response to the fruitless tree was to curse it because it was showing signs of being something it was not—prosperous.

In our daily lives we tend to have enough power and strength to make it through the harshest of storms and have an increased ability to bless everyone around us during our emergence from the cold storms. But on us walking out of the storms, we forget WHO it was that helped remain fruitful in hard times & we do not turn and bless Him FIRST.

CONSIDER THIS ON THIS DAY

During these last days of the year, take the first moments of each of those days and bless God. Not with your money, but with the first 10 minutes of each day.

make the next several days true gifts for God to check and be impressed by what He created.

CONSIDER THIS ON THIS DAY
moving God into your house

THERE ARE SEVERAL TIMES during a year that we feel the need to change some things in our days and in our lives in which we feel would make us look, act or even seem better. In the middle of changing and rearranging, we find that there is a pushback when the items we need to move and remove are people and they want us to remain in the same position. That is answered within a simple solution. But then the tough nut to crack would be the person we see in the mirror.

We tend to move everything into areas of our control and not allow God to clear up the bumps and bruise that we obtain in clearing out things so we can allow Him to move freely in our homes and in all areas of our days. If we look at Uzzah and David and the Ark of the Covenant, we see that David wanted to obtain the Ark after the Philistines needed to get it out of their country. Some folks want the power of God, but cannot handle all the things that come with having God in their lives. The Philistines had obtained the Ark by dominance and control and thought that they could have God in their lives as a token, an idol and a box to control. But after all things in their country started dying out and remaining sickly, they called upon the people of God to reclaim what was rightfully theirs.

The questions which arise in our lives, should move us to not only want to be right, but move and live in a manner that trusts all the power God will allow to be contained in our little homes and in our daily lives.

The questions are:

Am I truly worth being blessed continually and then living a "right" life to hold onto all the blessings God has for me?

Should I lose a few friends and family to be in a greater fellowship with God or should I just live in the moment and be satisfied with the daily grace He bestows in my life?

Can my relationship with God survive the bumps and curves in the path that He has set me on?

Some questions are ours and then we will receive the best questions from family members wanting to know:

Why we moved away from them?

Why we are putting God in front of everything and moving them out of the way?

And who do we think we are that we can act like church is the best place to be?

All these questions above are rehearsed in the David's wife Michal and her reactions to David attending "church" we the people he is supposed to rule over (II Samuel 6:12–23).

So, who should we listen to when it is time to move and make room in our live for God?

CONSIDER THIS ON THIS DAY
cheerleading yourself

> Reference Scripture: Psalm 23

SOMETIME DURING OUR DAY, we must take a moment to remind ourselves how we have arrived safe and blessed and unharmed. We do realize that there were moments when that one day should have been our last OR that one dumb decision could have destroyed our family.

Our remaining ourselves is giving into the fact that it was/is never by our own strength and power but always comes from God.

In Psalm 23 David gives us the words to empower us through those days that we are stumbling and struggling to regain our footing in our attempts to reach our goals. This time of the year is no different.

Looking back over the last 11 months we can see that God not only carried us, but provided several areas of escape and moments if deep peace—none of it coming from our inner power or design.

It is HE who sets us in positions to meet another challenge.

Be your own cheerleader today while reminding yourself of the reasons you worship, trust and praise the one God that will never fumble on any promises in getting you to your goals.

Raise your head up.

You are not alone in your storms and struggles.

This year is coming quickly to an end; how will you impress yourself and start off running in the next six months?

CONSIDER THIS ON THIS DAY

getting old stuff back

Reference Scriptures: Luke 11:1–13, Mark 11:20–26, Luke 6:25–45

WE HAVE BEEN GRANTED a life that is forward moving and attention getting by means of our talents, gifts, focus and desire to complete certain tasks.

We have been blessed with a great open fellowship with God, who in turns pushes us to become greater in this forward moving life. His fellowship is always positive, productive and pursuing.

It is always our need to hold onto things and people that do not fit our growth and those this which will cause us to truly become greater in this life.

But we keep crying about old things lost during bad relationships and how the enemy needs to give us our stuff back . . . why is there such a grab at old things when we serve a God who is willing and able to give us better if we keep moving forward?

In Luke chapter 11, Jesus' disciples take the time to question Him about prayer and being like other folks. Jesus' reply was to give them a model prayer and then directions on dealing with others in this forward moving life.

Not in none of the New Testament or in the Gospel, does Jesus say that He, the Holy Spirit or The Father (this is the Trinity) will reach back and give us OLD STUFF.

So why keep holding onto the past??

What is the reason to take large steps BACKWARDS in a forward moving life?

There are songs and those that will scream in prayer, "I want Satan to give me my stuff back . . . my old lover back . . . why?

This is where the scripture comes in about us asking "for the wrong things" and I see those songs and prayers directed in the wrong direction.

God has created us to be great individuals. In becoming great individuals, there must be a greater level of maturity and higher standards than what the world offers. Reaching for dreams, goals and understanding our purposes in this life does mean losing and letting go of some old stuff & some old anchors.

Choose to be better in all your days. Choose to keep reaching higher in God so you can get greater and better in all of your days in the middle of becoming that person He created you to be.

FRIDAY

Nothing is truly over until you have crossed the finish line

CONSIDER THIS ON THIS DAY

holding your breath

Take a deep breath.

That thing which is causing you to look at your stance in God and then the world cannot overtake you. Well, unless you allow it to.

In some circumstances, the pressures to adapt and overcome are not an easy find. This is where the virtue of patience comes into play. (Psalm 40) & (James 1:4) It is that taking a breath to allow yourself to regroup and refocus on the simple choices in stressful situations.

Not one person on this earth is above getting upset, becoming angry or frustrated to the point of blowing out a few "blue words" now and again. That is being human. The difference in the life of the believer is the choice to call on another believer for support. Not because you are weak. You call because you understand that there are certain strengths which come along with the aid of a fellow believer.

In Hebrews chapter 3, the writer begins by reminding the believers that they are a called-out people, separated from the world through the Hands of God. He details the reasons why we are counted worthy of being in the family of Christ through all His actions for the purposes of reconciliation.

There are those days when frustration and anger causes us to hold back our prayers and conversations with God. As if we can hold our breaths long enough and force God to move on our behalf without us trusting in the relationship or Him moving in on the problems and issues causing us so much grief.

Some circumstances and situations require cool heads (Proverbs 4), but then there are those situations which require brute force. This is where the writer shines the light on verse 3 and the need for each of us to pray / speak strength into the daily walks of our brothers and sisters; because we all need help on this Christian journey.

Holding your head up when you heart has been broken and you just cannot think you way out of dire situations is not a sign of hiding anything. It is the beginnings of you deciding not to quit on yourself and start believing that God is allowing you to go through some things to punish or berate you. Those circumstances and situation which are most difficult are there to show you that you are not alone in this life. You have believers you know who will not only pray for you, but will pray with you. And in some cases, they have the answers you need for you to get out of the storm.

Read Hebrew 3:1–14

Make this day the day you call that one person who has been on your mind and send up a pray for them while you are having that 3-minute phone call.

Small embers can start a huge fire in the life of someone struggling to get a word from God.

CONSIDER THIS ON THIS DAY

fractured friends

Ours is a life of hard journey's and tough decisions. Our changes come when we have certain people transition in and out of our lives on a daily basis. Those people are meant to fellowship with us. Their friendship is developed on a time frame that is designed to be limited, but effective on an ethereal basis.

Then there are those that cross our paths, interject into our very beings and fuss with us about stupid and silly decisions. There is no transitioning away from them; even those hours that they have gotten on our last nerves and have made us so angry that we cannot see straight. Not because they are correct at every turn, but the mere fact that they challenge us to become greater in our walk on this Earth.

In the 24th chapter of Luke, we find two friends on a walk after a heartbreaking event has taken place. They are walking, crying and fussing about the things that could have taken place and those things that should not have happened because of the positions of some of the people involved in all the events. They were fractured; physically and spiritually, but they stayed with one another. Their understanding grew when they realized that the one friend who encouraged and empowered them could create in them a desire to move from one low area in life and then journey towards empowering others.

Sometimes, being so distraught on past events we cannot see that person that fills us and creates a burning in our hearts calling us to look passed the problems that will arise from failed events. We all have great talents that are at our disposal. The reasons why we have not reached where we should be in this life is because of the people we keep holding onto.

Decisions need to be made concerning who is attached to us 20 years from now:

> Those who are meant to transition out of our days are those who are continually reliving schoolyard events and would like every day to be carefree and the responsibility of someone else.

> Those who are feeding into us and calling us to do better are not trying to kill us or deter us from reaching our goals.

All of us at some point in time need a little prodding to get us back on the paths of growing in strength and power.

Are you willing to humble yourself to break old and bad cycles out of your days?

Make this day the day you decide that living in static transition is just not enough.

CONSIDER THIS ON THIS DAY
fellowship, unity, & discipleship

Love is the primary mark of Jesus' disciples.

Fellowship—between the members of the church is vital.

In Matthew 18:18–25, we Read of the power that results from such fellowship among the disciples of Jesus. A paraphrase of those verses would Read something like this: The Lord Jesus said, "If two or three disciples of Mine are found in one place and have no disunity between them, but instead a unity like the symphony ("sumphoneo" (Greek) = agree) produced by several musical instruments playing together in harmony with each other, then I will be present in their midst.

And then, if they ask My Father for anything, it will be granted to them. They will have authority to bind the workings of Satan in any place on earth; and whatever activities of Satan they bind here on earth, will be bound at their source in "the Heavenlies" (from where these spirit-powers operate). Such believers will also have the power to deliver (loose) people who are bound by Satan on earth." The devil knows the amazing power there is in unity and fellowship among Jesus' disciples, but many believers do not know it. And so, Satan's main aim has always been to bring disunity among believers to make them powerless against him.

What power there would be in a home, if the husband and wife were one in spirit! Satan would never be able to overcome such a home! What power there would be in a church if even two of its elders were one in spirit! Satan would never be able to overcome such a church! Satan triumphs over most Christian churches and homes, because such unity and fellowship is not found in them. I am not talking now about casting out demons. Any

Believer, who has faith for this, can cast out demons in the Name of Jesus, single-handedly, as Jesus said in Mark16:17. This is reaffirmed when we Read in Matthew 7:22-29 of even unbelievers who cast out demons in Jesus' Name. But to bind the activities of Satan, to release people from the problems Satan has created for them is far more difficult. A Believer cannot do that alone. That requires an expression of the Body of Christ—and the minimum number of disciples that can express Christ's Body is two! Only the authority exercised by such a "body" can keep the powers of darkness at bay.

There must be at least two people at the center of every church who are totally united with each other. Satan will always target such a core seeking to split it up and divide it. If he succeeds, then that church will become powerless against him. But if that core keeps itself united, Satan will be powerless against that church. This applies to a home as well. In every church, there will be mature people as well as new converts—just as there are babes as well as grown-up children in a family. The babes may fight with each other, backbite, complain and gossip, because they have not understood the way of peace. Such babes will be found in every growing church. But they can never hinder God's work. A core of united elders at the center of a church can make it an overcoming church. Babes may constitute the clear majority of every church.

But God is always seeking to build up the core—both spiritually and numerically. It is this core that fights the battles against Satan and preserves a church in life and victory.

Fellowship in a church is more important than evangelism. In the parable of the lost sheep, Jesus said that the 99 sheep in the fold were "ninety-nine righteous persons who need no repentance" (Luke 15:7).

Who are the ones needing no repentance?

Obviously, those who refuse to look at themselves against the standards of God. In other words, they do not want to see where they are falling short; those who walk away and try to do things on their own and out of fellowship with God and His Children. Such people do not need any repentance, because they are constantly repenting of their sins. Such disciples have no problem becoming one with each other. If, however the 99 sheep in this fold were constantly fighting with each other and tearing each other to pieces, then the shepherd would not have brought that lost sheep there—for that sheep would be far safer on the mountains than within such a fold where it could be killed! Our churches must consist of "righteous people who don't need any repentance." Then only will our churches be places of healing and peace into which lost sheep can be safely brought in. The Lord leads His sheep into green pastures and beside still waters. The church Jesus builds is a place of peace. Lost sheep must be brought in only into such a church. Most churches are not like this, because their members are converts and not disciples.

CONSIDER THIS ON THIS DAY

trusting beyond friendship

SOMETIMES WE TAKE THE simple things for granted. We overlook them because we expect things to remain the same and in place. Well, that is if no one shakes the balance of things or upsets the apple court. There are some days when friend and family members think they know more about your life and the paths you are taking than you do. Even if they are 100% wrong, they still interject their thoughts without Reading the full context of your walk.

I have spent more than 6 years writing the daily Bible Lessons "CONSIDER THIS ON THIS DAY" and have enjoyed learning more about the Lord in the preparation of each lesson and my walk under His Grace. This year has been a strange and trying set of personal lessons for me in the areas of friendship, respect and character.

If we take those things that we hold dear to our hearts: our name, our character, our self-respect to be settled because we are adults, we would find out that we are standing on the wrong side of wisdom (Proverbs 4). If we would seek a lesson in all the things which confront us doing our daily grind, would be the best option in rising above those challenges.

In the 3rd chapter of Proverbs, the writer begins with the standards which will keep any believer from losing their cool and reacting in negative and unprofitable ways when sudden pressures of life arise. Just as the hurricanes travel from horn of Africa throughout the Atlantic Ocean seeking a body of land to bless and change, so does the trials offered by those who we call our best friends, family and the people who only know of us because we work with them.

TRUSTING BEYOND FRIENDSHIP

Sometimes we take the foundations of relationships to be the cure-all, but that is not the case when challenges are great and we need trust wrapped in grace to make it through.

As I reflect on the months which have passed this year, my personal challenges did not come from the people I know who don't like me, but from those I had put my deepest respect and love. But then I realized in the moments of those relationships fragmenting, that the ability to lean on God for answers and directions would allow me to keep those standards mentioned by Solomon in the beginning of this 3rd chapter. Though I felt heartbroken by the actions of several friends, my reaction was and is set in verses 5, 6 and 7.

Anger is a quick and hurtful emotion. Some of us are all too Ready to allow that emotional door to be opened and things flow from our lips which destroy our character, what our name means to others, and the respect people have for us and our stance as a Christian become shaky.

Though my friends and family hurt me deeply, I will still do for them. But one has to realize that the relationship with family and friend cannot be the basis for living a righteous life. That honor and place has to be set in and revolve / evolve in the fellowship with have with Christ Jesus.

Read Proverbs 3:1–10

Make this day the day you decide to make Jesus your central focus in all the issues you are dealing with.

After you have Read this, open up the text and Read it for yourself and see why trusting in God will not only get you through the trials, but increase your status with those who are seeking salvation. YOUR ACTIONS / REACTIONS DO MATTER

CONSIDER THIS ON THIS DAY

compromising your identity

> Reference Scriptures: Joshua 2:1–24, Philemon 1:10–25, Daniel 6:10–23

WHAT IS IT ABOUT you which causes people to watch all your actions so closely?

Is it your clothes, personality, charm, your money or is it the way you carry yourself which causes folks to stand up and take notice of you?

Having a close / strong relationship with God changes the behaviors and choices that we have toward life and who we choose to associate with. They all can tell that there is that ONE thing in you that is not resting in them. They want to know how to get it, but will not ask nor will they do what is required to find the peace that you have come to understand as a child of God . . . and when they cannot get it without having to give up some stuff . . . they will work their hardest to make you lose all that you have gained.

In the 6th chapter of Daniel, the writer gives firsthand accounts of the actions of those who were jealous of Daniel's relationship with the king and his God. And from all accounts, the relationship that Daniel had with the king wasn't first on his list of Earthly priorities.

In our pursuits to be known as great people, our treatment of what is important to us, must be prioritized. Daniel, Onesimus and Rahab all chose to make a distinct pattern of how their lives were going to be set in God and then in the world.

First—they chose to put God first.

COMPROMISING YOUR IDENTITY

Secondly—they chose to make sure that their personal foundations (morals and ethics).

Thirdly—they moved to set a standard for all around them to take notice of their personal actions / choices.

Ours is a life that is under a microscope. All things that we think about doing, must match up with our prayer life and the image that we give out to the world. If all the things do not line up—then we should call ourselves LIARS and move onto the next episode.

CONSIDER THIS ON THIS DAY

thieves in the temple #2

Some and most of the things we wish for, want and feel are adequate and right for our lives actually are not. They are not because of the purpose and personal intent behind our decisions. Poor choices and bad decisions in the middle of God working in our days will cause us to have to pay for those bad decisions a great deal earlier than we could have ever anticipated.

In the lesson, the exact same things take place, God is blessing the community and the community is listening, well except 2 families (the husbands) make poor choices and the wives agree . . . the first knowing the consequences and the 2nd showing no respect or regard for those things that are of God.

Does responsibility and accountability have a place in the church OR does all things fall on God?

Is it His fault that those who have called Him Savior fail and fall in life?

Do Christians get a "pass" from bad behavior and doing things outside the standards God has given?

As seen in the decisions by those in the reference texts, we can see that poor choices become those weighted demons which control our days and kill off our fellowship with God and hurt so many people who depend upon us to be that LIGHT at the end of their stormy days.

Read: Acts 5:1–10, Joshua 7:1–26

CONSIDER THIS ON THIS DAY

contend with or content with

SOME OF OUR DAYS are filled with so much strife and problems that we tend to overlook people in our lives and blame then for the failures that seem to have over—taken us. There is a course that we should be able to see, but that takes TRUST.

The best example to offer is the trials we face when we must deal with the people in relationships. This is a give and take that relies on the fellowship having the ability to be open and filled with trust. If one goes into a "love" relationship thinking that they must set up a way of escape, then that relationship has alReady been setup for failure.

Contend—in Biblical terms is the personal steps taken to dig in, find ways to keep personal and family faith standing strong and having the ability to see success where failure should have stepped in and won.

Content—in Biblical terms is that phase of life that the Believer has gotten to the point that they are not filled with the worry of what shall come, how things will turn out and who should take care of what

Following Christ takes some steep changes and a lot of giving up of things in life.

The questions are:

Is it worth it to give up stuff to follow Jesus?

Is the relationship I am in now worth pushing toward Jesus so that all things will fall in line?

Can I take God at His Word while I fight to prove to the world that being a Christian is not a waste of time?

CONSIDER THIS ON THIS DAY

In our pursuits of having a good and settled life, how much can we see ourselves giving up setting things on the right and correcting path?

Read: Matt. 6:25–33, Luke 3:10–14, Phil. 4:8–13, Daniel 1:12–20

CONSIDER THIS ON THIS DAY
thievery—rehab is required

Reference Scriptures: Exodus 16:1–20, I Timothy 6:6–10, Luke 17:12–19

AFTER MANY DAYS OF us doing things that we think will ensure our days on this Earth are great and good, we move to take shortcuts in order to accomplish things that require work and true effort. It is within our everyday that God contends with our attitudes and our wants, complaints and needy ways. But when do we open up and do right by just doing right?

Constantly, He blesses us and we take for granted that all He is requiring of us is fellowship. Never realizing that with honest fellowship the relationship grows beyond measure and then we are strengthened and blessed because we know Him a little better and we begin to act and perform a great deal better. The problem with us getting into fellowship with Him; effort is required.

EFFORT—a vigorous and truly determined attempt.

We all want to have a great spouse and great kids.

We all want to own a nice sized house that we can make into a home.

We all want a good and paid off vehicle with low insurance.

All of that takes effort, but somewhere in our communities the push to work and then gain has been put on the back table with the "get rich quick schemes" of the world and then the churches of God have adopted the concept that one can steal away those things that require effort, sacrifice and dependability.

CONSIDER THIS ON THIS DAY

Our lesson this week will open up the reasons why we need rehabilitation from our days, years and months of stealing and then falling short.

CONSIDER THIS ON THIS DAY

what we want is what we want

Reference Scriptures: Numbers 22:1–34, Acts 9:1–9

SOME OF OUR DAYS seem to be open with great blessings and others filled with hard lessons. As we have discussed over the last several weeks, it is our choices that causes us to either gain a great deal from God or fall repeatedly on our faces. The latter is more common since we seem to be hardheaded creatures.

In Numbers 22: 1–34, the discussion between the prophet and the king shows us examples of how easy it is for God's children to choose Earthly blessings over those items God can grant in our lives.

The prophet was alReady in a good position within the church and for all accounts; we would believe that he would have been in enjoyment to have opportunities to openly speak with God on the matters of His people. But when we run into people who could give us an immediate influx of cash and notoriety, we lose our minds and the purpose God had given us the positions we are in. In His wisdom, God moves out of the way so the education we receive will have a more permanent impact on our hard heads and chosen directions.

As parents, husbands, wives and leaders in the church, it is our drive to move toward God's divine plan to increase our standings in this life and lead others into greater fellowship with family and then in the church.

God's Will falls under the scope of Divine and Permissive

Divine Will = those standards and precepts that God has in place for the church to move toward.

Permissive Will = God's grace to move out of the way and allow us to fall on our faces and learn that those things that we want and do will not get us to that "good place" we thought that we should have.

Simply, if we would allow patience to work in our days, then we could see and understand God's design on our days, but our NEED to have things done immediately only slows the revealing of those blessings God has placed in our life's path. The good thing about God is that He is open enough to allow us to move away from His Hands to realize that we cannot make a good climb up our mountains without His help and direction.

CONSIDER THIS ON THIS DAY

turn the other cheek

> Reference Scriptures: Exodus 14:1–14, John 17:14–26, Job 13:15

IT IS AMAZING HOW some people will turn around and spit your kindness and help in your face as if it is or has been a bad virus.

Our reaction—Our reaction should be as our Savior says it should be, TURN THE OTHER CHEEK . . . not to allow them to use you, but to show them the side of God that is in you which will kill them with love & kindness.

In EXODUS chapter 14, Moses dealt with the same issues of helping people meet God to change their pitiful situation. But in dealing with God's selfish and hardheaded children, our steps should be as Moses' example shows—turn the other cheek and call on God to answer the issues confronting us concerning His children.

In John 17—is the preparation Jesus set in place for his demise and resurrection and our position in Him.

I am not telling you to forget their bad behaviors toward you, but forgive them and give them over to God and then move on with your life. Carrying them, their attitudes and their hard headedness will cause you to have bad health and your hair to turn gray early.

At some point in time, adults must be left to fall on their faces do they can meet God for themselves. The problem that stands in the way . . . parents working hard to keep raising 30 & 40-year-old children. The best out . . . cut the apron strings and turn cheek for them to see the God you have been praying for them to meet.

IN OTHER WORDS, get out of the way.

Give it all to God when you have run out of viable options and places to run.

CONSIDER THIS ON THIS DAY

a centered focus lessens the view of the storm

Yeah, tough days & rough people seem to make life a difficult climb. The middle section of any bad and rough day is the solace of the Lord.

He remains constant. He is affixed in His care for us and in His promises toward us:

1. So why focus on storms caused by others in our days?
2. Do they have any power to change or remove those blessings God has specifically created for you?

Within you is the power to move mountains and change the tides of raging seas, but one negative word from someone who does not . . . feed you, take care of you, hold you when you are tired, pay any portion of any bill in your house takes your focus from all the things you have prayed over and prayed on. But God remains faithful to keep you moving forward.

In Psalm 37, the writer explains several times that the blessings and protection from God is always in place, it is the focus of the Believer's faith that causes worry and disgust over the actions of those (friends & family) that makes good days bad and rough.

Find your focus.

Believe in all the talents you possess because they we created for your enjoyment first. Let all the naysayers deal with your Heavenly Father . . . you move around them & have a great day in the Lord.

> Read Psalm 37

make this day the day that you open up and trust God to carry you through rough days and scary storms. Some recognition of those things that are taking place in our days is alReady evident, but we tend not to exercise the natural talents we must discern when things are not appropriate for us to move higher and become stronger in God and in our daily walk

- Change is what happens to us from outside and those things that we do not have control over.
- Transition—is our inner response to the changes we are experiencing and over which we do have control.

MLK stated at one point in his ministry, "a successful man is never satisfied with the current state of his life . . . "

CONSIDER THIS ON THIS DAY

chasing dreams and purpose

During most of our days, we tend not to look back and study those things that we have gotten over and broken through because of the hurts and pangs that are associated with them. This is a problem that all may suffer from in one way or another. The best way to move and change the frame work and set patterns is refocusing.

Focus—is the ability to find a center line of interest in any singular activity and use that line to move into a clearer frame of thought and insight

---

Read I Chronicles 11:22–25

Desires, Wants & Needs are the different levels one deals with on a day to day trek. The strange happenings in not acting correctly on either can cause the individual to lose ground in maturation and pursuit of goals.

The other side of pursuing dreams and goals is the two cents that is always offered and most times is contrary to what the individual has been praying on and for—and will consider that nonsense

It is called being distracted.

Our need to become better pushes us to seek those things that will get us closer to our goals and dreams

Our wants are settled in the animal-like instinct of conquering and subduing. This is the drive behind one overcoming obstacles and detours in life to clothe and feed family and spouse.

The portions of our days that are visions and dreams are based and wrapped in those desires.

Some come to fruition.

Some that remain visions and goals never pursued or accomplished for one reason or another.

In 1 Chronicles 11, the text shows us that there were certain individuals (Benaniah = ben a nye uh) who desired to be as good as the king and wanted to move into a greater fellowship with Him. What is seen in each of them is their desires moved from dream to want to need. They fulfilled their needs through preparation and belief in their own talents and gifts.

Prayer, preparation and planning will get any individual from one level in life to another.

This is called being settled and focused.

The question remains—what is holding each person from obtaining and moving forward??

CONSIDER THIS ON THIS DAY

becoming the Christian you should be...

> Scripture References: Proverbs 31:1–31,
> 1 Timothy 3:1–7, 1 Corinthians 7: 1–16

IN THE SEARCH FOR a good life, we sometimes tend to sell ourselves short of all the talents that we have been given. In particular, women are given a tower of strength, which has been pushed down to what she may wear, how it fits on her, what size she may be and if she is sexy enough to be on a guy's arm (if he takes her out).

God has made a woman to be the "Help Meet" of the man He has created for her. The problem in becoming that SUPER woman... some settle for the first thing breathing and are angry, upset, disappointed, discouraged, disgusted and empty at the end of most days. And then the long days of not believing in their talents are if they have reached their true purpose and potential and did not know it.

The fact of the matter is this, IT IS MORE THAN OKAY TO BE SINGLE FOR A WHILE... there is not a man on this earth worth the salt in your tears, if he is not willing to lift you up on a daily basis, thank you for listening to him cry about nothing on most days and a few good things on the 12 really bad days that may cause him to want to give up... there is not any one person, who should rule over how YOU believe and think about yourself. Your self-worth is in the Hands of God and you have been blessed before you realize what you have and who you truly are . . . you do not need one single person to validate what has alReady been ordained from above . . . YOU were created to do super things through tough and trying times.

Most psychologists state that women are too emotional and cannot handle stressful situations and keep their self-esteem and self-efficacy intact . . . spit on that and keep pushing on as you have been doing.

To solidify your daily strength . . . Read Psalms 40 & 43 . . . . . there is Grace and Favor that are waiting for you and the Hope that we all have in knowing that God will not leave you in a void and unprofitable situation or heated circumstances . . . it is your choice to be the "wifey or the superwoman." . . . . choose this day where truly want to remain and be known as.

Ladies, in Proverbs 31, it speaks of the Woman that is behind the man. The Word shows how strong her character is and who benefits from her being that strong rock and tower for her husband.

Men, in I Timothy 3, it speaks of the role of the man as the "pastor or bishop" of his house. It details all the steps that should be taken to be the true leader and light of his house and captain in his life—not shaken by every wind that comes along. In Proverbs 31, it begins with Solomon speaking to his son, kings and a man named Lemuele about the failures that follow chasing women and drinking . . . they forget their parts in the roles of leadership and why their stance in God is the way is it.

In the woman being the backbone of that man, her actions cannot mirror his or cause him to stumble and fall. If you are his and he is truly acting as yours . . . be his . . . talk openly with him (not to him) tell him those things that you wish to obtain and how you want to be treated.

Respect and Honor only arrive when the when the entire house is clean . . . both of you have to talk to one another . . . openly . . . and all things spoken must remain between You and He (no my boys or my girls' thang).

Remember this, he cannot be great unless you are there to help him over his shortcomings and failures. NO MAN is an island.

In the man being the head of the home and house, he must be open and willing to speak and discuss all issue facing the house, family and relationship. Not one thing can be in secret as Christ leaves nothing to chance with us. The man must be available to answer any question or take up any challenge the woman is facing and requiring direction. In this area, the doors to respect, admiration and love towards him is open.

But if you are single—love yourself and learn of yourself, before meeting that new person. It is okay to be single in a world of broken-barely working relationships and half-promised/half-married couples. Be true to you and believe in all the things that have been given you by God.

CONSIDER THIS ON THIS DAY

all things that are precious

In this life, it is the little things that we do that can bring smiles to a person's face and brighten up their lives. Granting gifts or blessings to a person may be that one thing that changes the course of their days. But in this fast-paced world, even the strongest of Christians have become busy and blinded by the call of the Holy Spirit to bless those who we know and see are struggling to make it through the day.

The act of blessing or gifting a person is not always a monetary (money) present. It may be your time, an ear to listen to the person vent and / or a good "how are you doing?" may be that one thing to set their day on fire and bring them to the light of Christ.

Take a moment on this day to open the door for a stranger, speak to that co-worker you have been avoiding for weeks, call that friend you have not spoken to in weeks. Bless them with your presence or just send up a prayer on their behalf.

Gifting—is the open action of granting or bestowing a present or gift.

Blessing—the actions or words from a person granting favor, mercy or certain benefits.

Offering—a thing or something giving or contributed as an extra gift.

> Read: Acts 5:1–10, Malachi 3: 3–10, The Rich Young Ruler'
> (Matthew 19:16–30; Mark 10:17–31; Luke 18:18–30)

In both Acts and in Malachi, certain requirements were given and those requirements were not met. Nothing given was given with great weight or circumstances that would have caused pain in the homes of the child of God. It is the limitations that each individual place on the "gifting" and "blessing" that become the barrier to reaching new levels and greater fellowships.

In Malachi, the priests were not doing what they were supposed to do.

In Acts, certain people made a promise and failed to carry out their promises.

Within the context verses of the lesson, there are certain aspects of being a child of God that falls into our days and allows us to become greater or opens certain things up and allows us to "drop the ball."

What did you see that had taken place that could have been avoided?

CONSIDER THIS ON THIS DAY

get up and get up with determination

THERE IS NOT A time in our days where we have not fallen down, failed and had missed opportunities. But we survived to live another day.

The result of getting up is the experience of having fell is the resulting knowledge gained and unexpected maturation which takes place. Though all our experiences are different, the steps in getting up are similar.

In Proverbs 24, the writer describes the attitude and personality the believer should subscribe. These traits are the bases for calling a person just and righteous because they are based in selflessness. After the description, the writer then moves to the choices made by the believer when life's challenges come and the ability to believe in one's strength and power. He simply states that if the believer doesn't stand strong, the believer will fall apart and falter.

There are strong challenges that we face from day to day, which should cause us to walk away and quit this life of being a Christian. But once a person comes in contact with the Lord and has experienced His grace and mercy it is hard not to get up.

There is another perspective offered by the writer about the actions of the believer once they have gotten up. The actions of looking at those who live outside the standards of God and taking pleasure in knowing that they have fallen and did not get up. This should never be the attitude or accepted into the life of any Christian (Galatians 6:2), we should reach out and help them understand why we keep getting up (Proverbs 24:16).

Better said, "Because you have gotten up is not the end of the getting up, unless you help another who is struggling in the same manner as you."

> Read Proverbs 24:1–25

Make this day the day you choose to get up and then make a difference in someone else's day.

> "people will remember how you made them feel, not what you've done for them"—Maya Angelou

CONSIDER THIS ON THIS DAY

our testimony versus the spiritual manipulator

Reference Scriptures: Mark 10:14, Acts 13:44–51, Ezra chapter 4 & 5

IN OUR PURSUIT OF getting right with God and changing the way we are seen, there are some folk who truly believe that they know the best for us and can direct our days better than the directions offered us by the Holy Spirit. These people can be best explained through their actions and the way they work to manipulate situations and circumstances to best fit them and them only; they have Libertine-type personalities.

We all have our own attitudes concerning our personal growth and the well-being of our families. And those things have direct impact on our testimonies and the way our blessings and fellowship with God flows—daily.

As we grow in God and learn more and more of His Word and then apply those things to our daily grind, we seem to fair better after we have given our day to Him and move to allow our testimony speak for all things that we do—that is—we choose every minute to live for Christ and speak or not speak to keep our heads above the silly conversations and arguments at work or school, which have nothing to do with getting folks saved and keeping us in right relationship with God and our family. Then that Libertine steps in and gives us their two cents on "what thus says the Lord" and gets the scripture wrong and out of context and gets us to the point of getting upset or going along with those things they say just to keep the peace.

OUR TESTIMONY VERSUS THE SPIRITUAL MANIPULATOR

But who are we to serve to make our lives and days better?

In Mark 10, Jesus gave specific instructions to the church concerning our offering people our testimony and telling them about the Gospel of Jesus the Christ and walking away from them when they rebuffed our profession in Christ.

Why is it so difficult for us to leave folks alone and continue being directed by the Spirit toward a higher standard in God?

Do our friends and family offer better sanctuary while we are in the middle of a personal crisis?

CONSIDER THIS ON THIS DAY

who are you and what do you show yourself to be

> Reference Scripture: II Samuel 9:1–8, John 15:1–9,16

Relationships can take deep cuts into the development of friendship and trust in what should take place in the future.

If one person puts in more than the other without receiving anything outside of the joy of putting a great deal of work, mileage on the car to see the other person, money spent to give gifts for the sake of showing how they feel about the other person, then where do the principles of the other participant in the relationship begin and end?

Principle—as the rule, belief or standard that governs the actions of an individual.

As we have been Reading over the past weeks, the standards that God has given to us, is often reminded to us by the Holy Spirit in an attempt to grow us into the spiritual people that we should be and allow us to have that distinct ability to HEAR from God's Spirit when He is calling us to do the right and correct thing.

In some of the early days of a relationship, one party takes on the responsibility of trying to set the foundation and then quickly burns out, because the other party's standards are those of "take" more than "give." We work to lower our standards to make the other person happy instead of requiring them to grow with us.

Example: phone calls—the daily phone calls go from being answered to falling into voicemail with the excuse, "I was busy" or "my phone isn't working right." This is a new decade and phones just do not fail to operate like they did 5 & 10 years ago.

driving—love is one thing, but infatuation is that item that would drive one person to spend all their cash on gas to fill their car to drive to "the love of their life." If the woman of the relationship is doing more driving than her "boyfriend", "man" or "significant other" just to see him . . . questions should arise. Nesting is supposed and is designed to fall on the male species.

The foundations of relationships have been so eschewed that no one reaches back and asks what the standards should be or other issues of "not wanting to be alone" and "why can I not find a person who will treat me like the Lord does or will." Those things come to failure because we lower our standards just to have a warm body around us; no matter the cost to our financial standings and to our character.

In our reference text, David has opened himself up to be ridiculed for his actions toward his enemy's child. But his principles were based in God's Word and His actions in David's life. It is always easy to give 100% of ourselves and then overlook the return work from others based on love giving them in the hour of need or in the matter of principles

CONSIDER THIS ON THIS DAY

best gifts and simple talents

OUR DAYS ARE GROWING shorter as we have the tendencies to look back at "the old days" or "that's what we used to do" in our process of accomplishing tasks or enjoying time with family and friends. Those are some of the things which matter most to us. Some are the most valuable things in the world to us and we tend not to give our best or simply "just enough" to make the situation end or that person feel better.

Value is defined as anything having worth or substantial meaning.

Talent is defined as one having a natural aptitude or skill

Read: Matthew 25:14–29, Isaiah 55:1–11, Galatians 6:1–7

We value the time spent at church because those are the people who make us feel important.

We value most of our days at work because that is where our rewards originate to pay bills and accumulate things.

We value the days that we attend either place and neglect HOW we can visit either.

Then look at our talents at both places is limited by our belief in what we WILL not allow ourselves to do. We tend not to step out of our comfort zones and trust God on the other side of the unknown reactions and results.

Within each of those days that we face, certain opportunities avail themselves for us to either uplift those around us or make certain circumstances better for the people in our circle of influence. The question arises from our speech, daily communications and our actions toward the people we place certain value.

> Read James 3:5–14

We tend to blast them in public.

We tend to curse them concerning simple matters.

We tend to break them down on any occasion and opportunity.

We tend to lie to them in order to control them for our benefit.

Still the case remains that these are the people and places we value the most in our lives.

It would be reasonable to say and think that those people that we hold a great deal of love and respect, are in fact the best gifts we can ever receive in our lives.

Dealing with money (talent) is one of the hardest portions of our days. We can either use it to gain "stuff" or use it as a tool and means to develop longer lasting blessing for ourselves and others and not get so emotional about not having it and blame or accuse other for the lack of talent to utilize it correctly.

Husbands—our wives are the gifts that God has created specifically for the man

Wives—your husbands are created gifts, which are to lead and protect you into a better standard of life

Our Children—they are that miracle which two persons can procreate as a reminder of the Grace that God has given to us

Jesus—He is the greatest gift that God could have ever planned to give to us through his death, burial and resurrection

Husbands—will curse their wives and call them names they would not call their pet dog

Wives—will tell all the secrets to her friends, which should stay between the married partners

Children—well—they will mimic the actions of their parents . . . the circle begins

Jesus—We all forget about him and use the Lord's name in vain while joking or watching a good basketball game.

These are those gifts that we are supposed to hold in high regard

And yet, WE TREAT EACH OF THEM LIKE DIRT.

That is the best talent we tend to lean on in moments of frustration and gift people with the worst that we can give without realizing that all our actions have direct and lasting impacts on those we deal with and those who are just watching us.

Let us take today as the first day of the rest of our lives

Let us tell our family and our friends that we appreciate them above all the things that we have incurred and caused to happen.

Let us change the standards on how we value those in our lives by loving them openly and often in public.

Pray for our children, husbands and wives by holding their hands and pat them on the back and tell them that they have done a good job.

Sometimes, things are not always about US . . . but how we handle the situation.

This is where the value of all our talents come into play.

CONSIDER THIS ON THIS DAY

throw caution to the wind

FACING A NEW DAY brings about those who will tell others how and when they can let go and release all things to God. This is just a bunch of nonsense. Certain titles and length of time worshipping in a certain place does not usher in any kind of authority over the Holy Spirit nor how and when one can open up and praise God.

Psalms 100 & 150 tells all of creation to praise and worship the Creator with all the power that resides in our beating hearts.

CONSIDER THIS ON THIS DAY

attitude and posture = success

Judges 3:12–30

We all feel that we have a certain purpose in this life. As most would say, "a calling." But how do we see our way clear when moving toward God, while dealing with the people in our days, the clowns that cause confusion and anger at work, those who seem to distract when Sunday Service has alReady started.

How do we hear from God and remove those distractions from our minds?

Righteous Indignation—typically is a direct reactive of emotion of anger over perceived mistreatment, insult, or malice. It is that stuff that makes us upset because it is not in the will of God and you feel / know that the action will upset or anger God.

In the lesson text, Ehud (A—Hood) was not supposedly the best person to choose as a Judge, but God can use anyone and anything to move His agenda in our live forward.

Success of any kind is based on our attitudes and posture during those moments of anger and frustration.

CONSIDER THIS ON THIS DAY

an about face can change failed directions

> 2 Chronicles 7:12–16

IN SOME FORM OR fashion, we have heard this scripture shouted out in prayer and in the church and never took time to see the history and background into why the Lord seeks for His Children to seek prosperous directions and agendas.

Leadership is one thing, but having an ability to step down from high places and take the backseat, one can learn a great deal of things by watching and listening. It is the example that gives those around us a clearance to speak and act at a certain level. Everything based on what they see in us. Solomon had taken a place in the congregation as worship leader and gave a prayer of supplication to the Lord in the sincere hope that God would bless the Children of Israel and continue to be with them no matter their choices. After all his heart-felt praying, Solomon found himself without a word to say when God appeared to Him the temple. God heard him and made mention of his prayer and desire.

Examples are those good things we see in others and then work to add them into our daily routines.

God hears all that we say to Him. The things that slow Him down from acting in our days are our inability to be faithful to Him and our families. God requires those who worship Him to be prepared to meet Him at His level and on His time. In chapter 6, all the people were at the correct place, the problem is they did not expect of God to be in the very place He created.

Verse 14 is the answer God gave to Solomon as a corrective measure in the setting of boundaries and getting the children of Israel to fellowship with Him all over again. No one person is above another based on person acts or merits: someone has gifted them that position and the image shown to others is what drives them away or pulls them in closer.

Leadership is a direct example. It offers insight to how the person is away from the group, the church or the job. God sets a standard and still requires that same standard in all of us. This is the mindset we should have in dealing with folks. Our standards must be in line with God's for those who are not quite right and for those who can smell their own behinds and believe themselves to be great.

But all things remain in the hands of the individual and his / her choices.

CONSIDER THIS ON THIS DAY

going at it alone

But there are those people who know us, walk with us, cry with us and get angry at the same things we do. These are the people that we enjoy having around. These are the people that inspire us to do better and reach for higher goals.

If the choice has been made to follow Christ and all the examples He has left, then GOOD friends are attribute that should be acquired and cherished. In Matthew 8, he speaks of the fellowship of GOOD friends being a benefit when all know Christ and are open to make request based on the need of the friend, the pain of a loved one and the need of the family and church and the whole time directing all things to God and not dishing out dirt on any subject. These actions allow you to see the power of God within His children and then in yourself.

United Prayer is the catalyst that will change habits, behaviors and the foundation of personal faith. Good company does not corrupt good morals, it strengthens them.

Yes, the Word does make it known that the devil is like a lion . . . seeking who he can destroy. The Word does not tell us that the devil is seeking a group of people, but that one person that will try to do things on their own and out of the strength of the fellowship. Yeah, I paraphrased . . . but there are only certain instances that individual success can be achieved and that success is only for that person. But when there is success by a group, it not only grows the power of the group . . . it makes all around stand up and take notice and then join into the group ----adding strength to the group.

I do know that we have friends and associates that are known from childhood. At some point in time, the idea of a childhood friend should be dropped because we no longer are dealing with child-like issues. The enemy would like us ignorant and looking backwards. There is no growth in the future if the only thing thought about is recess, playgrounds, 8th grade dances, old high school loves and things left in the halls of a school you never return to.

This makes you distracted.

This makes you a target.

The devil may at times attack, but his attack fails when each person in the group remembers WHO is in the center of the group and WHO is the power source that allows the group to move as one. It is the familial draw of the group which gives singular focus to the problem and the solution.

Sometimes.

Sometimes.

Friends from the past that offer no positive incentive in your future MUST be left to be exactly what they are PAST FRIENDS. It is time for you to link up with stronger people to acquire and obtain those things God has gifted to you and your family . . . old friends can say hello to you at the class reunion and then you can tell them how good God has been to you.

Make this the day that you open up and trust God to put GOOD people in your days that will inspire, encourage and push you to reach your full potential.

CONSIDER THIS ON THIS DAY

when an earthly man becomes successful

THE DESIRE OF A man is to have a loving woman, a house, a car, good job and family. In the middle of those desires comes personal standards and work in the effort to do some nesting to achieve those goals.

Nesting is that ability to set things up and maintain them through hell and high water. The male bird begins nesting long before he finds a mate for life. Though some species of bird move from one mate to another—he still does the work it takes to set up the nest, feed the offspring and ensure the female has all that she needs until the offspring can fly and fend for themselves.

In no way am I suggesting that the Human Male Animal (Earthly Man) should bounce from one woman to another and just populate the Earth, but it seems to be the norm of today's society.

Ephesians 5:25 states that a man is to LOVE his wife in the same manner as Christ loved the church. This means that this earthly man must take spiritual steps to ensure that all things about and for and to this woman are done above board. He is always willing to bend over backwards for his woman (wife) and not expect a thing in return. He is to seek the best things for her and his house. This means to walk away from all those single and wrong thinking friends that would seek to end his relationship with his woman and keep his mind in a state of "seeking to find a woman that his friends think is best for him to bang, sleep with, hang out with, make his baby momma, or just a conquest. HE MUST HAVE A DESIRE TO RAISE HIS STANDARDS IN LIFE and become better than what he was raised in and what he sees in his neighborhood. His desire in life must be more than what he can do this week and this month.

The Earthly man must change his focus to looking toward a twenty-year future.

In taking on a wife, there is this weight and challenge that only a few can bear. Those who quit are not mentally prepared to give of themselves and not think in the area that they should come first in the relationship. Sometimes in order to receive the best gifts in life, one has to be open enough to make sure the blessing (the wife) in his life is comfortable and happy before he is. The she will bless him in the way a wife is supposed to—freely and lovingly—and not in the cycle of being just physical pleasure, but out of a need to be one with her husband.

Nesting in the earthly male was a mainstay before the choice of being a Godly-Man in the life of his children and wife. The desire to get an education and have a home setup before the seed is dropped is put on the back burner with thoughts that one can change / catch up / build a home after the "wild oats" are sown. This pushes the earthly male away from the call of God and into a need to fit in the world's definition and acceptance of a "get-by man."

Now the choice is to become a "get-by man" or "baby daddy" and be satisfied in life that their children are left to struggle and suffer their entire lives because they do not have the love of their father . . . nor the direction needed for them to achieve better in life. There is not one woman on the Earth who is satisfied with a man who cannot hold a job for more than 3 months and asking her to step up and pay the bills (this is a get-by man). The power and strength to carry a family . . . it takes an earthly man with a vision based in God and those standards that are set for a man to be GOOD for his family ALL OF THE TIME—WITHOUT FAIL.

Yes, there are mothers who rear children to become better in life, but the blessing of that male—parent fills the hole that is left and is something a woman cannot fill; no matter how many hours she works. That child still misses the father. The hole that is left is filled with hate and anger.

Psalm 1 states that a man is blessed when he makes his delight in the Lord . . . this means he wakes and prays for his wife and children and his job to ensure all things are in line with God and he meditates on those things he has learned in church and from his parents in the pursuits of having his house stand in hell and high water.

WHEN AN EARTHLY MAN BECOMES SUCCESSFUL

Yes . . . the life of an Earthly man is filled with deep struggle, but it changes when he lays his eye and heart on God, puts his wife and kids on his back and takes them (not as a burden) as the treasure they are and will move them above the trials, temptations and terrors that are associated with this world. He brings them to the top of the mountain and gives them God in everything that is his family and home.

CONSIDER THIS ON THIS DAY

do you know what you know?

Some information and choices that we have gained come to us in the areas pick one and desire the other. In the area of our salvation, Jesus makes the simple offer to have open access to God.

In the Robert Frost poem . . . the question of pursuit in the right order plagues all who have ever walked the Earth. So why is it so hard to do and choose the right things in life?

The Road Not Taken
By Robert Frost 1874–1963 Robert Frost
Two roads diverged in a yellow wood,
And sorry I could not travel both
And be one traveler, long I stood
And looked down one as far as I could
To where it bent in the undergrowth;

Salvation is defined as deliverance from sin and its deep consequences. It is a preservation from the harm that should be attributed to the individual for the job done in obtaining so guilty a life.

All Have Sinned	Romans 3:10	Romans 3:23
Sin's Penalty	Romans 5:12	Romans 6:23
Christ Paid the Penalty	Romans 5:8	
Salvation through Faith	Romans 10:9,10	Romans 10:13
	Eph. 2:8–9	

In John 3:16, Jesus states that all who would like to believe on the Son may be saved and receive the gift of Eternal Life, but in the next verse, we can see that salvation is as open as rejection.

With no middle ground, why is it so easy for a great deal of us to overlook the responsibility of accepting Christ and moving toward a better life?

Is living the Christian Life too much of a burden because it requires all to change certain habits and behaviors to move into a higher fellowship with Christ?

Can you lead someone to Christ and feel comfortable doing it?

CONSIDER THIS ON THIS DAY

what we want is what we want

SOME OF OUR DAYS seem to be open with great blessings and others filled with hard lessons. As we have discussed over the last several weeks, it is our choices that causes us to either gain a great deal from God or fall repeatedly on our faces. The latter is more common since we seem to be hardheaded creatures.

In Numbers 22: 1–34, the discussion between the prophet and the king shows us examples of how easy it is for God's children to choose Earthly blessings over those items God can grant in our lives.

The prophet was alReady in a good position within the church and for all accounts; we would believe that he would have been in enjoyment to have opportunities to openly speak with God on the matters of His people. But when we run into people who could give us an immediate influx of cash and notoriety, we lose our minds and the purpose God had given us the positions we are in. In His wisdom, God moves out of the way so the education we receive will have a more permanent impact on our hard heads and chosen directions.

As parents, husbands, wives and leaders in the church, it is our drive to move toward God's divine plan to increase our standings in this life and lead others into greater fellowship with family and then in the church.

God's Will falls under the scope of Divine and Permissive.

Divine Will = those standards and precepts that God has in place for the church to move toward.

Permissive Will = God's grace to move out of the way and allow us to fall on our faces and learn that those things that we want and do will not get us to that "good place" we thought that we should have.

Simply, if we would allow patience to work in our days, then we could see and understand God's design on our days, but our NEED to have things done immediately only slows the revealing of those blessings God has placed in our life's path. The good thing about God is that He is open enough to allow us to move away from His Hands to realize that we cannot make a good climb up our mountains without His help and direction.

Read: Numbers 22:1–34, Acts 9:1–9

CONSIDER THIS ON THIS DAY
greatness defined in you

> Reference Scripture: Matthew 20:20–28, Genesis 12:2, 2 Samuel 7:9

IT IS NO SECRET that all of us crave to be on top of things, become successful beyond those in our circles of influence and accomplish that one thing which would set us apart from the crowd. And all of this could take place.

The items which stops us from having great relationships, getting the top ratings at work to garner that 8% raise and having good credit is based on the actions of sacrificing those behaviors, old friends and often brothers and sisters to reach the higher levels of talents and gifts we refused to use.

In Matthew 20:20–28, the writer details a brief encounter with a mother, who saw greatness in her children and wanted them to be at the highest levels she could possibly bring them. She brought them to Jesus and made her requests known. But in turn, Jesus didn't respond to her, but her sons—why?

We all have been pushed, cussed and fussed at when we have fallen short of certain goals and made bad choices which continually delay those successes we desire. Our parents can only take you so far in life. After that the questions rest at the feet of the individual, who should either step up, openly make the choice to take on the challenges of drinking from that cup of struggle to success or cower and return to mediocrity.

God has gifted each of us with great talent and the power to use it in a manner that will not only put us ahead of the crowd, but will allows us to teach & train others to get and gain as we are.

GREATNESS DEFINED IN YOU

Make this day the day you step to Jesus and affirm your inheritance and blessings toward greatness.

CONSIDER THIS ON THIS DAY
taking what is yours

> Reference Scripture: Joshua 1:1–9, Psalm 115:16, Matthew 6:26

Does it not seem kind of strange when we run into people who are educated and talented, yet they are still living a mediocre life and do not have the drive to do anything within their talents and gifts?

We heard it time and time again, the only thing which holds an individual from achieving and obtaining is that on little thing that rests within them. No matter how much encouragement given, they seem to bask in the glory of not doing so they won't be called a failure.

Is that the one thing holding you back, someone calling you a failure?

In the first chapter of Joshua, we discover that Moses had died and the children of Israel were without a leader for the first time in 40 years. Not only did they not have a leader, their access to God was cut short. But God had made provision in the case something did happen to Moses. He had created the man of Joshua—attitude and all. He was chosen by God.

God had a conversation with Joshua in the first nine verses of this chapter and gave him all the tools he would require to take all that was promised to the children of Israel. After having repeated the promises that He had told to Moses, God filled Joshua's ears with them again and then added, "be of good courage." What is it that hinders and retards our flow forward in life, even after we have prayed and cried and then God answers?

Ours is a cynical life. We ask for things then we refuse to take the steps or make an effort to achieve the littlest of successes because of fear someone will see us leaving their circle of influence or stuck in the pattern that if God blesses us, we have to wait on family to make the decision to follow us as we follow God's call in our days.

Look at it this way, Psalm 115:16 tell us that all things on this Earth were created by God for human consumption, protection and control. But failure arises because the lack of courage and the ability to believe in self.

The time has come for us to make the decision to either believe in God and His promises or to walk away and accept being a quitter. Courage is that animal that will force you to run straight ahead and only question your steps once you have reached your goals. If you have prayed and thought over certain paths of action, what is causing you to drag you knuckles in pursuit of what God has granted in your life?

If God has promised it, where is the failure originating?

CONSIDER THIS ON THIS DAY

taking what is yours

QUESTIONS:
In Matt 6:26, Jesus directs those who are listening to Him to look up in the skies and see exactly the birds in creation are doing.

"Look at the birds of the sky. They don't sow or reap or gather, yet your Heavenly Father feeds them. Are you not more than they?"

If God has an invested promise to keep to us, how do the birds demonstrate how to actively wait on the Lord?

What is the difference in active waiting and passive waiting?

What are you waiting on from God? Is it active or passive or just procrastinating?

Read Joshua 1:1–9

What phrase did God repeat to Joshua over and over? Why did He emphasize this phrase?

After your morning prayers and getting Ready for work, what task has God been pressing you to be strong and of good courage to handle?

What are the challenges waiting for you if you decide to take the step toward taking what is offered to you from God?

Do you feel that living under God's rule is too large a task?

What do you require to motivate you in reaching the task and believing all things are in God's control?

CONSIDER THIS ON THIS DAY
leave the past behind

Reference Scripture: Joshua 1: 1–9, Philippians 3:1–14

THERE IS A GREAT deal of looking back taking place in the days of the Christian man and woman which limits their thoughts, dreams and steps into the future. But in looking back, they tell a forward-thinking God to increase their territory when neither individual is Ready to look ahead at the obstacles, opportunities and overwhelming blessings waiting for them.

A great deal of good relationships falter and die out because one party is looking in the rearview mirror every single day and speaking on things they wish they could have stopped or removed in a prior relationship; killing off all hopes and dreams of the partner, who may want to create positives all day long.

Here it is in a nutshell: Looking at the past is supposed to be a glance and not a staring contest.

If the individual spends a great deal of time looking back, wondering and hoping that something from the past would miraculously change and the negative days will all disappear. God doesn't work like that and neither should you.

When we strike out to become successful, one must accept the process, the problems and the perils ahead to mature and become stronger. At the end of the acceptance, when the arrival at the doorsteps of success that is the time that one needs to look back and smile at the things in the past because they will not be a need for a sequel.

LEAVE THE PAST BEHIND

In Joshua 1, the story is told of the children of Israel leaving the past and stepping into a future without Moses and now had to look to Joshua to see how he was going to handle his first steps into the future. We can consider that there were some in the crowds who did not like where the path was going to take them. All they wanted was the things that are familiar to them, in this mindset lives procrastination and complacency.

The problem with walking away from the past and leaving it behind is the fact that you have left days of chaos and hell in every place you been. Or maybe you passed up on your responsibilities and decided to miss out on opportunities in order to recreate some event from the past. All of this makes it both emotionally and physically difficult to let go and move onto the area in life God keeps calling you to.

This is the area where trusting your faith in God is either a bridge or a cliff.

It is not a moment in time, but days where you sit and put off and begin to think and believe life has failed you. Life has not failed you one iota. You are failing to live your life to your full potential because you want to remain "child-like" and not fully step into the calling God has placed inside you. You want to be lead and pacified into a leadership role in life. In Romans 8:37, the Apostle Paul reaffirms the faith of the church by letting them know that the past is just that, the past and each member has accomplished great things and refuse to accept their inner strengths.

This is the day where trusting your faith in God is either a bridge or a cliff.

CONSIDER THIS ON THIS DAY

accepting all deterrents

Reference Scriptures: Proverbs 1:1–9 & 4:1–12

HERE WE ARE IN a world where the bold Christian is scared to live and speak the word of God, because someone may be offended, either by the actions, the beliefs or the just hearing the word and having it invade their souls.

Here we are in a world where being politically correct is supposed to be the norm, but that changes the moment one person screams that they feel violated by a belief system they say is outdated.

In basic terms, these folks are fearful to live to a higher standard.

The term to fear the Lord simply means to live in dRead and awe of His total being. This causes the believer to have a desire to become more and more like the Lord is.

What the Christian should realize is that we serve a God who is omnipresent, omniscient and all powerful. He is not a fairy tale that can be wished away because some say that they refuse to believe in a God they cannot see or hear from. That is their choice. Our choice is to live in respect for all that He can do and that He will do in the lives of all creation; whether they believe in Him or not.

In Proverbs 1 & 4, Solomon makes the claim of how to approach and then live in fellowship with God, with an open mind and a child-like heart. It is in that approach the Christian should take the correct steps in learning of and hearing from God as if it is the beginning and we are learning things

ACCEPTING ALL DETERRENTS

all over for the first time. But that takes discipline and this world is so far removed from a disciplined life that it is almost laughable.

Here we are in a world that does not take God seriously, but wants the blessings of God to be there because they can eat, breathe and work. Every creature on the planet can do that. The difference between the believer and the non-believer is the believer tends to take on more of God's character and walks in less fear of the world.

For you to get passed the point you find yourself today, is to begin to realize that you have nothing to be fearful of and all things to gain. The world will tell you that your socio-economic status limits where you can and cannot go. The word of God tells you that you are more than a conqueror and that you can do all things any time of the day and any hour and in any minute that you decide to put feet to the faith that you claim you possess.

CONSIDER THIS ON THIS DAY

it is fun being saved

Reference Scripture: Phil. 1:3–21

WITH ALL THE THINGS we have to deal with wrapped up in "what else could go wrong" on a minute to minute routine, we tend to take our position in Christ for granted. Yes, life is hard. But that is only on occasion and based in the choices we make that create some circumstances that spin out of control.

Yet when we stop, take a breath and then realize that all of our steps are ordered by God. The repositioning of your feet for your journey and the taking of a good deep breath in the process of lowering of our blood pressure allows us to look toward the Heavens and thank God for another chance.

In the 1st chapter of Philippians, Paul and Timothy make every effort to detail the joys they receive, not only from knowing the people in the church at Philippi, but revel in the idea that they are going to see them again. But the strongest thing that is written is in the words, "in every prayer I make concerning you, I pray for joy." Not many people we know will look past their own struggles and ask God to bestow joy into the lives of those they care about; let alone those folks they do not see on a day to day basis.

Paul continues to detail the things that the church will face, when he compares it to those negative people he has encountered on his own Christian journey. In short, it is hard on some days to remain a dutiful Christian when you are bombarded by those who refuse to study the word, ask God for clarification of those things others have spoken into their lives with certain twists and turns added where it relates to the fellowship between the believer and God.

It is the fellowship which allows the members of the church to mature in the word. Herein lies the main issue with a great deal of "christians"; some only want to accept things that they alReady know and think is the total sum of Christian Knowledge. It is difficult to speak joy into the life of a person who alReady thinks they know it all (Proverbs 4:1–12).

The fun part of being a saved comes in the continued knowledge of the Holy Spirit constantly feeding us, taking care of us and then leading and teaching us how to walk better in this world in our preparation for the next. In this letter, one should experience the epiphany that all of this will end and the life we now lead is totally for the purpose of getting all the people we can to see the happiness that comes when living a life for Christ is taking and walked without worry of the day when all of this passes on. In short, it is better to live in expectation of meeting Christ in a face to face; rather than worrying about the stuff that will be left behind (Phil. 1:21 & Gal. 2:20).

No one can do your life better than you.

But when it comes to living a joyous life in Christ; that walk cannot be alone. We are social animals and crave distinct social intercourse in our pursuits of a good day. When we are wrapped in Christ, the fellowship of a brother / sister solidifies the activity of the Spirit in our days (Matt. 18:20).

CONSIDER THIS ON THIS DAY

it is fun being saved

Reference Scripture: Phil. 1:3–21

QUESTIONS:

What is the main reason why you come to church?

Is the knowledge that God will continually work for your good reason to become complacent in coming to church?

How do you think gaining a better understanding of Christ and the history of the Early Church will aid you in your Christian walk today?

Since we know Paul was in prison in Rome, why do you think his central focus was on Christ? Can we say he was afraid to die, bored or just writing letters to pass time?

Does his wanting the best for friend and family ride higher than his situation?

Does it not seem crazy for a person to wake up in the mornings, knowing they will have a rough day, yet you see them with the biggest smiles?

I asked this to ask you, where does your joy lie, in a good check with 33 hours OT, your favorite team winning the big game 6 years in a row or your partner treating you MORE than special every day?

Happiness is defined as a state of being cheerful, happy or in good spirits. (feeling)
Joy is defined as a state of mind and an orientation of the heart. (behavior)

CONSIDER THIS ON THIS DAY

taking responsibility

AS A PERSON WHO makes the statement claiming to be a Christian, it should be my main objective to live, walk and talk in such a way anyone who sees or hears me in a crowd, can recognize THAT CHRIST JESUS IS IN ME.

If, IF I become stress and act uncharacteristically out of turn, it's no one else's fault but my own. The devil did not make me do it. It wasn't caused by hormones, lack of money or car problems.

If a person calls themselves a follower of Christ all aspects of their days must align to that testimony.

One cannot be afraid to claim the trek they have chosen

I must be better and stronger than the people around me. I MUST BE THE SALT in my community.

I claim Christ Jesus on this day.

(Romans 1:16)

CONSIDER THIS ON THIS DAY

the symbol of your worth

Let's start off with this, "what do you consider the image of your self-worth?"

During all of the emotional stresses from the events of the last 15 months, which have caused the loss of life, the injured at heart not being able to find justice and the future direction of this country falling on the lines of repeating history.

It is as if the lessons learned from the past have not taken hold in any manner in the minds of God's people. Yet, some desire to seek varying avenues of worship while placing the Creator in a box until all parts of earthly history are justified as being right and correct (Exodus 20:4).

The concerns of the church have not over-shadowed the screams of society to worship a flag, a movement and the move to keep a distinction between God's people based on pigmentation and financial standings. In this attitude, the church as a whole-should realize "silence is not golden."

Luke recorded the actions of Paul in the 17th chapter of Acts and how he approached the desperation of the masses of people on Mars' Hill in their seeking to cover all the things they had placed in front of knowing and understanding that there is only one true God and that there is no roundabout way in worshipping Him.

One thing we should notice is the distractions which are placed in front our relationship with God causes the believer to lose focus on Heavenly standards and then choose those things shouted out in the world as being more important.

There are some who long for the "good old days", not realizing that most changes from those destructive things of the past were left behind for a good reason. In short, not all things from the past should be engrained into the future. Some days and sometimes some folk need to grow up and see that God has created all of His Children to do and become better.

Now if the symbol of your worth is based on a flag, an incident or a movement, which caused others to suffer in any way . . . those things, should be buried with the past (Romans 14:13–23).

The strangest thing about the subject of Idol Worship doesn't seem to bother the average Christian and their pursuits to hold up a flag, while not showing the love of Christ above all things. So, set is the Conservative, Evangelical and Liberal mind in placing their emotional desires above those things Paul had addressed on Mars' Hill so long ago.

The image of our worth should be more than a flag, a cross with the image of a beaten man, a covered tomb and a crowd of people chanting hurtful words at the funeral of a fallen soldier. The image of our Christian walk should be resemblance to the standards Christ gave as being the greatest commandments of all in Mark 12:30–31.

Read Acts 17:22–31

CONSIDER THIS ON THIS DAY

think before acting

MOST OF OUR DAYS seem to steep & endless, uphill climbs.

The ability to counter this is with planning, preparation and good advice; which centers on the people we allow to feed into our lives.

Proverbs 24 gives us directions on how to be wise in our choices of friends, associates and enemies and when to listen to each of them.

It is nothing like falling on your face and have the same people who gave the advice to you, ridicule you behind your back. This is where active wisdom comes into play. USE all the knowledge you have gained so far & then bring it all to God in prayer—sifting through all the advice and desires you have to be successful.

Yeah, you may fall. But you will get up again and again and again.
YOU ARE NOT A QUITTER.

Read Proverbs 24:1–16

Make this day the you trust in your ability to climb your mountains alone and with God's Hand guiding you.

CONSIDER THIS ON THIS DAY
silence isn't a portion of praise

IF WE THINK ON the days which have passed us by. Some carrying trials. Some carrying pain and grief. And yet others dragging misery, stress and fear. None of them have overcome us and destroyed to the point that we had lost hope and given up.

If we consider those days that we held up our heads and walked boldly into the new day. I say it's those new days that we realized God was with us through all those negative times.

In Psalm 61, David leaves the query answered with a song of shout and calls all who love God to open their hearts and mouths to make that noise no other can be gifted . . . joyful praise.

If you would consider that one day that car could have caused you to die in an accident or that day you felt so out of place and ill, God healed and blessed you beyond what you thought would take place.

I say, MAKE A JOYFUL NOISE

nothing has been promised that HE cannot deliver.

Make this weekend the time you open up your heart, mind and mouth and really make that joyful noise of thanksgiving to the Lord.

www.ingramcontent.com/pod-product-compliance
Lightning Source LLC
Chambersburg PA
CBHW071240230426
43668CB00011B/1520